MILLS TRANSFORMED

Stories of northern mill regeneration

MILLS TRANSFORMED

Stories of northern mill regeneration

John Hudson
Publishing

Neil Horsley

Published by John Hudson Publishing
22 Stratford Grove
London SW15 1NU

First published 2025

ISBN (hardback) 978 1 7385400 0 6
ISBN (eBook) 978 1 7385400 1 3

British Library Cataloguing in Publication data
A CIP catalogue for this book is available from the British Library.

Typeset in Circular Pro

Edited by Sarah Enticknap
Indexed by Auriol Griffith-Jones
Page layout by Matthew Wilson / mexington.co.uk
Printed in Europe via Akcent Media Limited

Cover Lister Mills, Bradford.

Back cover Gibson Mill, Hebden Bridge.

Title page Lister Mills, Bradford.

Dedication

To Mum – Anne Horsley (1929–2023) who was for ever asking “How is that book of yours coming on?”

Contents

Foreword

Charles Smith

Historic England

England's textile mills were once the workshop of the world. From the late 18th century onwards, they drove forward the Industrial Revolution. They triggered technical innovation, stimulated new trade and transformed the transport network. Silk, cotton and woollen production shaped the landscape, economy and communities of Greater Manchester, Lancashire and Yorkshire. Thousands of mills were built, and that heritage remains fundamental to the history and culture of these places today.

Sadly, following the demise of the country's textile industry in the second half of the 20th century, the north's historic mills are rapidly being lost. Historic England research, in collaboration with the University of Salford, tells us that over half of Greater Manchester's historic mills have disappeared since the 1980s. Those across Pennine Lancashire and West Yorkshire tell a similar story due to disuse, neglect and fires.

Yet, we have evidence that investment in mills can kickstart economic and social renewal. The successful Ancoats Urban Village in Manchester is centred around reinvention of its enormous 19th-century cotton-spinning blocks. The University of Huddersfield has embraced and reused canal-side textile buildings to forge a distinctive educational built environment. The charity-run Leigh Spinners Mill has become a focus for bringing people together, offering community, sports, arts and cultural spaces in the town.

There is so much potential still untapped. These distinctive, character-filled buildings can accommodate many more wonderful residences, workplaces and cultural facilities. Whether shops, gyms, theatres or spas, almost anything is possible in a mill. The vacant space they contain could accommodate around 42,000 new homes, or host 280,000 new jobs. At a time when local authorities are struggling to find space to accommodate

Houldsworth Mill, Stockport.

Dalton Mills, Keighley.

economic and housing growth, mills provide a ready-made solution on brownfield land.

As the development of our towns and cities becomes increasingly homogeneous, the north's distinctive industrial branding will likely increase in value. Mills can contribute to how the north is marketed nationally and internationally to prospective investors. From Bradford to Burnley and Wigan to Wakefield, they offer inspiring places where people can live, work and relax.

Importantly, we know that mills really do matter to people. A recent YouGov poll told us that 89% of adults believe mills are an important part of England's heritage, story and character, 85% do not want to see historic mills demolished and replaced, and the majority think they are as important to save as castles and stately homes. Through passion and creativity, alongside collaboration between public, private and third-sector partners, they can continue to serve at the heart of communities.

Historic England welcomes Mills Transformed as a highly important contribution to efforts to preserve and repurpose mills. Supported by a magnificent and inspiring collection of photographs, the book showcases restoration case studies and offers expert and practical insights into what makes a successful mill renovation scheme. While the heyday of mills as powerhouses for textile manufacture may seem a distant memory, this publication gives us hope that their best years as powerhouses for growth may yet be ahead of them.

Charles Smith
Policy Director
Historic England

1

Introduction: Mills and hills

I think it's very important to protect history and culture. What I love about the area is its industrial past and the way the people are reinventing the old mills. They're being looked after, respected, and therefore become part of the living landscape.

Sally Wainwright, playwright[1]

Walk anywhere in rural West Yorkshire and the chances are it is not long before you encounter a mill. At some point on your walk, it is likely you will find yourself heading down a Mill Lane, passing gentrified weavers' cottages, crossing a fast-flowing stream, walking past a proud chimney with its mill now converted to apartments, glancing at the remnants of a mill pond and then on up the steep hillside path. All without a second thought. Mills are so ubiquitous and such an integrated feature of the landscape it is easy to be oblivious to them. They are not so much *part* of the landscape but *are* the landscape.

Sadly, a similar walk in many peripheral northern towns will have many of the same features but all too often the mill will be derelict, decaying, neglected and marooned, alone in a fly-tipped wasteland.

Woollen, cotton and silk textile mills were the foundation of the Industrial Revolution and as much a part of our national heritage as churches, cathedrals and country houses. Mills were the catalyst for technical

Legram Mills, Bradford.

Dalton Mills, Keighley.

innovations, rampant entrepreneurialism, integrated industrial manufacturing processes, the labour movement, international trade links, investment institutions, rail and canal networks and the establishment of multiracial communities. Mills were responsible for place-making in northern towns and cities across Greater Manchester, Cheshire, Lancashire and Yorkshire. In short, they were the backbone of wealth creation in Britain in the mid- to late 19th and early 20th centuries.

The scale, grandeur and ambition of mills is unsurpassed. Visit and gaze at Salts Mill which, on completion, was the largest building in the world, containing the largest single room and which manufactured 18 miles of cloth each day. View the chimney tower at Lister Mill, dominating the Bradford skyline, or marvel at the sheer size of Dean Clough.

However, there are still more than 660 mills in Lancashire and Yorkshire which are empty or under-used. Many mills are under threat – over the last decade more than 100 mill fires have occurred in Bradford alone.[2]

This project, like so many, began during lockdown. I found I suddenly had spare time on my hands and the chance to walk, explore, think, worry and revisit old interests. I began photographing parts of West Yorkshire, fascinated by the rugged, uncompromising scenery, and became increasingly drawn to documenting mills and their dominance of the northern landscape. It was difficult not to reflect on their former lost grandeur and think about the people who built and worked within them.

Derelict mills are all too often used as a lazy illustrative short-hand symbolising the deprived industrial north. Too many national media articles on economic problems in the north are accompanied by a black and white photograph (always black and white) of a derelict mill or a vista of mill chimneys. The words 'satanic' and 'dark' will usually appear in the opening paragraph. To some, mills summon

up smoke-filled valleys, cramped back-to-back housing, cobbled streets and poverty. All things 'north' in fact.

A number of years ago, close to where we lived, a developer secured planning permission to build a housing estate on a former mill site. As a publicity stunt, the then TV celebrity Fred Dibnah, the go-to demolition guru, was employed to come and 'drop' the mill chimney at an appointed time. All the local residents turned out, waited for what seemed ages, watched the chimney collapse, looked at each other as if to say 'I suppose that's it then', and trudged back home. The developer clearly thought this publicity event was a great success, symbolising the discarding of the old making way for the new. When I now drive past the estate of Noddy houses shoe-horned onto the site, all I get is a sinking feeling and a wish the mill had been left well alone.

But there are some isolated good-news stories of people who have brought mills back from the dead, and given sufficient local and national political will, these could be models for further renovations.

As the book shows, there are many examples of mills being renovated and repurposed by inspiring people; life-affirming stories of the vision, grit, determination and perseverance of people who have undertaken successful mill restorations, often at great emotional and financial costs. Clearly everyone who restores a mill invests something of themselves in the endeavour. If such case studies could be replicated at scale, there are considerable opportunities to create quality housing, workspaces and jobs, while avoiding encroachment on the green belt.

As a result of conversations with a number of mill owners and renovators, the idea emerged of an illustrated book mixing photographic images and supporting text, which would bring to life their insights into the process of mill regeneration.

So, the book has three aims:

1. To celebrate the restoration and repurposing of industrial mill buildings in the north of England.
2. To tell the human-interest stories behind a number of the 31 separate mill renovation case studies visited.
3. To draw together common themes, insights and practical lessons as to what determines a successful mill renovation scheme and how further schemes can be developed.

The book will first consider the importance of mills, why they need to be preserved and the opportunities they offer. An overview of how mills evolved and their architectural characteristics has also been included to provide historical context.

Finally, based on the interviews and discussions with mill renovators, commercial developers, architects and public agencies, we will draw conclusions as to what actions can be taken to encourage further mills to be transformed.

Opposite Woodhouse Mill, Todmorden.

Below Mill and gas holder, Huddersfield.

2

Why renovate and repurpose mills?

Unfortunately, all too many textile mills lie vacant, are semi-derelict or remain under threat of demolition. Greater Manchester has lost over a thousand of its historic mills (48% of the total) since the 1980s.[3] For many in the property sector the view still prevails that textile mills are historic relics from a bygone era which are too expensive and difficult to convert to other uses.

Why then do we need to take steps to preserve, renovate and repurpose our mills? What are the arguments for taking positive steps to regenerate our abandoned mills to create modern spaces in which to live and work?

Mills – Why they are important

Mills are towering landmarks defining the landscape of the north and its industrial and architectural heritage. The scale, grandeur and concentration of mills in Yorkshire and Lancashire is unmatched anywhere else in the world. Mills dominate skylines and define communities. Local people often have an emotional bond to mills – as nostalgic connections to the workplaces of previous family generations or monuments to long gone industries and trades.

Although mills are a physical embodiment of the north's industrial heritage and wealth, they can also make a valuable contribution to economic activity. Mills are malleable and can adapt to changing times and economic requirements. They can change function over time and can be reborn accommodating unforeseen uses. Like old houses, 'they can adapt to changing times, they can survive economic downturns by slipping into states of almost suspended animation, living on long enough to be rediscovered and restored'.[4]

In summary, disused textile mills need to be regenerated and repurposed because

- According to Historic England, in 2021 there were 688 vacant or underutilised mills in Yorkshire and Lancashire, which if redeveloped, could create 42,000 homes and 84,000 jobs. Mills therefore have a vital role to play in the reuse of brownfield sites,[5] thereby reducing pressure for further greenbelt developments (**Fig 2.1**).

- Public opinion is strongly in favour of mill renovations. According to a YouGov survey, there is overwhelming public interest and support for saving mills: '85% of England's population do not want to see the demolition and replacement of mills, with 79% in the north of England saying they wanted mills to be considered for new housing, offices and public amenities before constructing new buildings'.[6]

Fig 2.1 Derelict Grade II listed mill, Midland Mills, Bradford.

- Mills play a unique role in place-making. Mills often act as local landmarks, dominating the skyline, and like church spires are focal points defining the character of a place.

- Local people often have an emotional attachment to mills as places where their relatives were once employed. According to Andy Burnham, mayor of Greater Manchester, 'These buildings are an important part of our industrial legacy – the original Northern Powerhouse'.[7]

- In terms of townscape and industrial heritage character, many people find mills aesthetically pleasing: 'Mills have windows of domestic proportions and domestic details which help to give a dignity rarely found in other industrial buildings.'[8]

- Mills are centrally located in many cities and towns and are close to amenities and transport infrastructure. They are often located at the heart of both urban and rural communities.

- Mills are often in close proximity to water – becks and rivers – and offer attractive riverside views.

- The extensive open-plan floorspace arrangements found in mills can be subdivided and adapted to accommodate a wide range of uses.

- Buildings with industrial heritage features have, according to one developer, a 'charisma and character' not found in more modern buildings. Many property buyers buy in to the concept of living in a historic building conversion incorporating modern facilities, close to town and city-centre amenities. This is an aspiration tapped into by one property developer – Capital & Centric – in their marketing campaigns: 'Duplex loft apartments in a 200-year-old piece of Mancunian history. These are homes that ooze industrial character, with exposed bricks, timber beams, high ceilings and huge windows that soak the apartments in light.'

- Office tenants, especially in the creative, digital and tech sectors are attracted to mills due to their history, distinctive character and 'distressed utility finish'. Many are prepared to pay a premium for a mill environment 'offer', including being part of a community of businesses, as opposed to being located in bland office buildings on business parks on the periphery of urban areas.

- Basic mill refurbishments can also provide low-cost workshop and storage space to incubate start-up and early-stage businesses.

- Mills often occupy large sites with potential for car parking or other on-site facilities.

- Regenerating vacant mills can secure much-needed income for local authorities, as empty listed buildings are exempt from business rates.

- The renovation of mills contributes to decarbonisation targets. The production and transportation of materials used in the construction of new buildings accounts for around 9% of all global emissions. A retrofit approach to mills, as opposed to their demolition and replacement with new-build properties, greatly reduces carbon emissions. The sheer scale and stone construction of many mills also means they are especially difficult and expensive to demolish.

In the words of William Gaunt, joint owner of Sunny Bank Mills, 'These beautiful buildings lend themselves perfectly to adaptation to a multitude of uses and preservation for future generations to enjoy.'[9]

Mill residents and tenants

Clearly, mill renovations will only happen if they provide a product that meets the needs and requirements of end-users – residents and tenants. Having stated that people are attracted to living or working in mills with industrial character and heritage, what is it about these buildings that people find attractive?

The following are the views of an artist and a business tenant who both occupy space in Sunny Bank Mills, Farsley, and residents of Lister Mills, Manningham, Bradford:

It wasn't so much that I chose a mill specifically, but a combination of factors meant that I ended up here. The cost (I could afford it), the location (I could get to it), the availability (there was a studio I could apply for), the reputation (Sunny Bank Mills has a great reputation as being a supportive centre for artists, makers and creative businesses, and has a fantastic gallery that shows some really interesting work). So, I applied and pestered a little bit, and luckily, I was able to get a spot! I know that there is a shortage of suitable and affordable studio spaces for artists, so I consider myself lucky.

Before I got a studio at the mills, I worked from home mostly (aside from a brief stint in a temporary space in a disused office building) and I was very keen to find a community to be part of, rather than working in isolation. The community is great, I love having my art friends and colleagues around me. We bounce ideas off each other and support one another. We can also offer each other advice, and plan events together.

I like that my studio is on the top floor of the old spinning mill, and there are huge windows on both lengths of the building, plus more skylights above. The natural light is fantastic for a painter. As you can imagine, I find it important to be able to see my colours in natural light.

I know that some of my fellow artists and makers have got a lot of inspiration from the heritage of the building and the architecture and history. I know that there are some old weaving looms here that can be used by weavers, and that's a lovely thing, to have that link to the textile history of the mills.

For me, I like to look out the window at the parts of the complex that haven't been developed yet, as I love a romantic ruin. The downside of having a studio in a historic building is that it can overshadow everything inside it. People are so in awe of the still visible traces of history that they can sometimes overlook my work that is inside it, that I'm trying to show them!

I don't think there are many artist studios that are not in old, repurposed buildings; at least I can't think of any that aren't in old factories or warehouses, or mills. So, with it being almost a ubiquitous arrangement, I don't know if this would be visible or influential in an artists' work: I think that's an interesting question. I am not conscious of the age of the building making a particular difference to my work but I expect that in a modern or purpose-built studio I wouldn't be able to afford the rent to be there in the first place. So maybe the difference for me is in being able to have a studio at all, and in that case it would be back to making work at home, and making smaller and less ambitious work, and feeling a bit isolated.

It feels good to be part of a community of people reusing old buildings that were derelict and unloved. I am all for the regeneration of old mills, and I'm really glad that the Gaunt family got Sunny Bank Mills (Fig 2.2) *back into a thriving, living thing. A friend of mine who used to live in Farsley has been amazed at the transformation over the years. I think everyone locally feels proud and there is this buzz over the mills being this leisure/culture/business destination; and I know that some people are super happy that popular TV shows get filmed here too.*

Helen Dryden, artist

I've had a number of offices down the years but for me this is by far the best place I've worked. It's the combination of the mill's character and history and the presence of other creatives that go hand in hand with the design side of our business. Compared to one of those faceless office park locations we could have gone to, the mill provides a far better location and creates the right image for our customers. I also think that being based here has fostered our creativity – lots of interesting businesses have moved into the units near us and we've ended up doing work for some of them. There is a real community here and the chance to have chats which generates ideas. The presence of the art gallery and the events which take place are also part of the benefits of being here. Old mill sites obviously weren't built with car parking in mind and this was an issue, but they [the owners] have now addressed this by creating additional spaces. I really enjoy coming to work here.

David Whitworth,
Brainstorm Design Consultants Ltd

I was born and brought up in this area and lived half a mile away, until we moved here. As a child I saw the mill when it was working and saw its demise. I worked with various campaign groups to get it reused. When it was renovated we thought we had to put our money where our mouth is and bought a flat and have been happy here ever since.

Velvet Mill resident

The building itself is an icon for Bradford. It's visible from whichever direction you approach Bradford so people see it and think, 'I'm nearly home'. When it was becoming derelict it gave the community a real down feeling – you felt everything was bad and going wrong. When it was done up it really raised people's hearts.

Third-generation Manningham resident

Constraints preventing mill redevelopments

So, given their potential and the demand from residents and business tenants, why do many mills stand empty and mainstream developers show little interest in developing them? The constraints preventing mill regeneration projects are as follows:

- Market demand – many mills are located in traditionally weak property market locations where occupier and investor demand are limited or non-existent. Low rental and capital values often make schemes uneconomic.
- Structural condition – a mill in a poor state of disrepair can be regarded more as a liability than an asset due to the scale of the potential renovation costs and the fear of 'unknowns' emerging.
- Issues such as difficult topography in many rural areas, poor access, limited car parking, flooding potential, the potential for asbestos to be present, etc all make mills unattractive to developers.
- Limited on-site space or flood risk issues can necessitate the mill's ground floor being used for car parking, thereby reducing the number of residential units which can be created, impacting on the scheme's viability.
- Adaptability and design issues can be major constraints – for example getting sufficient natural light into the middle of buildings with large floorplans.
- Uncertainty and risk factors – the state of the building and the costs involved in renovating it will only become apparent when work gets underway. As is the case with any historic building renovation, the challenges to be dealt with will only become fully apparent once construction works have commenced.
- Costs – the upfront costs can be substantial and difficult to predict accurately given the size and complexity of historic mill buildings.
- The level of resources required to renovate large mill complexes is beyond the capacity of many developers.
- Compared to the cost of a normal building renovation, mill conversion can be at least 40% higher.
- Timescale – many mills have a minimum two-and-a-half-year build/renovation time.
- Securing listed building consents and planning permission is a time-consuming and expensive process.
- Decreasing availability of public-sector gap funding to help meet abnormal costs.

Fig 2.2 Old Woollen, Sunny Bank Mills, prior to renovation.

DOORS
KEPT
USE

Obviously, the costs of each scheme will vary greatly and be dependent on the condition of the building, abnormal costs, proposed end users and their specifications, and so on. Soaring material costs and inflation levels have also recently greatly increased the costs of schemes. Although inflation has started to reduce, anecdotal evidence suggests the cost of building materials still remains high. However, to give a broad indicator, the Oldham Mill Strategy consultants assessed mill redevelopment costs in November 2021[10] as being

- Construction costs of between £1,300 per sq m and £1,900 per sq m.
- Professional fees at 7% of construction costs.
- Finance at 6% of development costs.
- Sales/legal and marketing costs at 3% of gross development value.
- Developer profit normally 15–20% of the gross development value. However, the report adopted a higher figure of 28% given the upfront investment and risk associated with a mill conversion.

Any affordable housing or local infrastructure contributions would be additional to these costs.

Clearly there are major hurdles to overcome with many mills that are currently vacant and in a state of disrepair. However, as the case studies contained in the book demonstrate, such issues are often surmountable. Before examining these solutions in more detail, it is worth spending time considering how mills evolved and their unique heritage and architectural characteristics.

Lister Mills, Bradford.

Sunny Bank Mills

Sunny Bank Mills in Farsley was founded in 1829 by a group of local weavers and grew to be one of the world's most important fine worsted mills. By the 20th century, the mill was one of Leeds' premier worsted spinners and weavers employing up to 900 local people.

The manufacture of worsted cloth ended in 2008, leading to the closure of Sunny Bank Mills. Two years later, William and John Gaunt, sixth-generation family owners, began renovating the mill complex to create local employment while preserving the industrial heritage of the site. A master planning framework was developed to repurpose the mill buildings in order to create office, specialist retail, gallery, workshop spaces, café, bar, archive facilities and artist studios.

The Gaunts' original vision for Sunny Bank Mills has been adhered to with a focus on renovating individual buildings, creating commercial space, and recruiting tenants, which in turn generates income enabling the redevelopment of other mill buildings and parts of the site. Selective demolition of buildings with little or no architectural or historic value has taken place to create space for new developments and improved access and car parking. The cornerstones of the mills' development has been its focus on cultural regeneration.

Sunny Bank Mills has built up a critical mass of over 100 business tenants and is now the single largest creative industries hub in the Leeds conurbation, attracting 500,000 annual visitors to the complex. The scheme has been self-financing, with over £4 million

Left William and John Gaunt.

Below Sunny Bank Mills exterior.

Right Millspace.

Below Old Woollen mill before restoration.

Below right 1912 mill.

re-invested in the mill site since 2010. No public grants have been received for capital works. The mill has been featured on national television, being the location used for the filming of *The Great British Sewing Bee*, while according to local property agents the regeneration of Sunny Bank Mills has led to an increasing demand for residential properties in Farsley village.[47]

According to John Gaunt, 'Our regeneration of Sunny Bank Mills is rooted in the community and heritage of Yorkshire's wool industry. I love the energy, skills and passion that so many people bring to the mills.'[48]

Holmes Mill

Holmes Mill is a Grade II listed former cotton mill, built in 1823 for James Thornber & Co in Clitheroe, Lancashire.

James Warburton, mill owner and local entrepreneur, has, since 2015, developed Holmes Mill to create a multi-million-pound leisure complex which is home to

- A Beer Hall with the longest bar in Britain (105ft long with 42 hand pumps!).
- Bowland Brewery.
- The 1823 Spinning Block Hotel – a 39-bedroom upmarket hotel complex with restaurant and bar.
- Bowland Food Hall – indoor market including delicatessen, patisserie, bakery, restaurant and local artisan organic food.
- Bistro, Bar and Grill.
- Everyman Cinema.
- Office workspace.

Heritage aspects of the mill have been incorporated into the design, including the restoration of the 1910 Clayton, Goodfellow & Company horizontal engine, located in the Beer Hall. In some areas it has proved necessary to replace the original cast iron columns with steel to support upper floors of the mill.

This large-scale listed mill redevelopment has brought buildings back into use which have been empty since the 1970s, regenerated the centre of Clitheroe and created 180 jobs.

Left Bowland Brewery.

Below Beer Hall bar.

Opposite The Spinning Block and Boiler House

SPINNING BLOCK
SPINNING BLOCK
HOTEL
BOUTIQUE BEDROOMS
FAMILY ROOMS
SUITES
BISTRO BAR & GRILL
EVENTS
FUNCTIONS
BISTRO
HOTEL
BISTRO BAR & GRILL
THE BOILER HOUSE
HOLMES MILL

Right Food Hall.

Below Incorporation of engine in Beer Hall development.

BOWLAND FOOD HALL
THE BEST OF LANCASHIRE AND THE BEST OF BEYOND
BREWERY
BEER HALL
ENGINE ROOM
LIVE MUSIC
EVENTS
FUNCTIONS
WEDDINGS
BISTRO BAR & GRILL
BEER HALL

Dean Clough

My vision for Dean Clough was to create 'a practical utopia' combining culture, commerce and enterprise.

Sir Ernest Hall[49]

Dean Clough is a vast complex of mills in Halifax, stretching for over half a mile and spanning 22 acres. The mills were built for Crossley's Carpets over a 20-year period beginning in 1840, and became the world's largest carpet factory. At the height of production 4,000 people were employed across 16 buildings, totalling 1,250,000 sq ft.

Production ceased in 1982 and Dean Clough was subsequently purchased by Ernest Hall and Jonathan Silver for a sum rumoured to be below a million pounds. According to Ernest Hall, a successful textile entrepreneur, the mills had a 'daunting sense of emptiness'. Hall's vision for Dean Clough was to create 'a practical utopia' combining culture, commerce and enterprise: 'I realise that the process of designing fabrics and running a business was a creative process similar to composing music or writing poetry and satisfyingly productive'.[50]

Although Hall and Silver had great respect for each other, they found working together difficult. According to Silver, 'I was tiring Ernest out with my enthusiasm, arrogance and energy'.[51] Jonathan Silver left the venture

Below left Vintage sign.

Below Walkway.

in 1984, selling his shares in Dean Clough to Hall and later went on to purchase and transform Salts Mill.

Dean Clough is regarded as a model cultural regeneration scheme which has evolved organically into a major arts, business, design, retail, hotel, leisure and education complex. One of the founding principles of Dean Clough has been a strong commitment to supporting the arts, and the mill is the home of theatre companies IOU and Northern Broadsides, the 300-seat Viaduct Theatre, galleries, collections of original art works and artist studios.

Over a 30-year period the mill buildings have been reduced to approximately 600,000, sq ft, commercial space has been created and 150 business tenants attracted. Plans are currently being developed to convert vacant space in C and D mills into 118 residential units, creating a mixture of two- and one-bedroom flats. The management and evolution of Dean Clough is now led by Jeremy Hall, son of Ernest Hall.

Above Dean Clough.

Right Abandoned TV.

DEAN

Likened to a communist-era East German engineering works ...

Ponden Mill

Ponden Mill near Stanbury is a Grade II listed building constructed by John Heaton in 1791. It is one of the earliest and best remaining examples of a cotton mill built in Yorkshire. In 1803 the mill had 25 employees and by 1811 housed 16 water frames.[52] The photograph shows how to the right of the original building a number of extensions were added to house the steam engine and boiler when the mill was converted from water to steam power. A chimney was constructed in 1825 and the building extension in the foreground was added in 1893.

The mill was bought by Barry Brookfield in 1973 who created a factory shop and café visitor attraction. As a result of the demise of the Ponden Mill retail chain, the mill was closed in 2008. Within a week of its closure the mill was vandalised, with the roof, floor and internal wiring all stolen. The mill remained derelict for a further six years prior to its sale.[53]

Owners Richard and Barbara Trainer, who are both archaeologists, have painstakingly regenerated the mill to create an events space, bespoke accommodation, café, bar and campground facilities. A number of imaginatively themed accommodation options have been created within the mill grounds, including the Frank Lloyd Wright-inspired 'Falling Water' cabin and the 'Pondenrosa', a coal wagon converted it into a western covered wagon.

Left Richard Trainer.

Right Ponden Mill.

Falling Water cabin.

Ponden Mill.

3

The evolution of textile mills

The development of mills is essentially the story of the Industrial Revolution, with rural cottage industries being totally transformed by entrepreneurialism, mechanisation, steam power, cheap labour, availability of building materials, access to new raw materials such as cotton via the British Empire, new sources of investment capital, and manufacturing innovations. Added to this mix, the development of canal, rail and turnpike infrastructure collectively provided the foundations for the creation of large-scale textile mill manufacturing operations throughout the north of England.

The design and construction of mills was determined by the interrelation of textile production process requirements, machinery and power innovations, and advances in construction techniques. Many changes in the scale and layout of mills were driven by the increasing size and complexity of new textile machinery – for example, spinning mills evolved to accommodate larger spinning mules, while weaving sheds were developed to house power looms.

In this chapter we will give a brief outline of the evolution of the textile industries and their influence on the design, building and development of individual mill buildings and subsequent integrated mill complexes.

Loomshops

Prior to the Industrial Revolution, many farming communities relied on hand weaving to provide an additional source of income. In the mid-18th century, textile production was based on either a domestic system, where raw materials were worked into finished

Fig 3.1 Weavers' cottages, Haworth.

Fig 3.2 Loomshop, Colne Valley Museum.

products by family groups and sold into the marketplace, or by the 'putting-out' system, where a manufacturer would buy raw materials and 'send them out' to waged outworkers, often tenant farmers, to spin and weave in their own farm or cottage dwellings.

Throughout West Yorkshire it is still common to see groupings of weavers' cottages either in pairs or short terraces. It is thought that they were built as speculative enterprises by merchants or manufacturers to provide both rented housing and workspace for a waged labour force.[11]

The first example of buildings being designed specifically for textile production is that of loomshops created to accommodate woollen weaving. Weaving would be undertaken in a purpose-built third-storey garret above a single 'two-up-two-down' cottage (**Fig 3.1**). Large, unobstructed, well-lit spaces were required in order to accommodate three or four looms, a single fireplace and storage space. Cottage ceilings would often have to be raised to accommodate the height of the loom. Such workshops would house a workforce which was often no more than a family or extended family grouping.

Larger single loomshops could be built over rows of cottages which maximised daylight for the operation of looms by long rows of mullioned windows called 'lights'. Access to such loomshops would be through a trapdoor or a separate external stairway, enabling the loomshop to be operated independently of the cottage accommodation below. Loomshops also offer the first evidence of 'taking-in' doors – doors inset in the gable walls of the upper floors of a mill through which materials could be winched from the ground below on delivery and finished products despatched on completion (**Fig 3.2**).

Hand looms were passed down through family generations, and being bequeathed a loom was a sought-after and much prized asset given its ownership provided the opportunity of a regular if modest income. The act of being bequeathed and inheriting a loom is from where the term 'family heirloom' is derived.

As the industry grew and the workforce increased, larger-scale loomshops were constructed separate from workers' accommodation. These would vary in height between two and five storeys, but would be of narrow rectangular construction due to the issue of providing adequate daylight within 'deep' buildings. Traditional construction methods were used, with wooden floors supported by timber beams and stairs incorporated at the gable ends of the building.

Non-domestic loomshops would be 5–6m deep with square windows on both sides of the building. In many cases they could be quite large – the loomshop at Chapel Lane in Addingham is three storeys high, 12 bays long and housed 62 looms in 1829 (**Fig 3.3**).[12]

Early cotton mills

The term 'mill' was derived from corn mills and came to denote a building used for industrial cloth manufacture. Existing corn mills were often adapted for the purpose of textile production, while water-powered corn mills also provided a model for the mechanics of power transmission within early textile mills. Mills were constructed with several floors and were just wide enough to accommodate machines without significant loss of daylight from rows of large windows along the building façade.

However, by the late 18th century, mills grew in scale and numbers due to increasing levels of production resulting from textile machine innovations and their ability to harness water as a power source. The first cotton mill in Yorkshire was Low Mill at Keighley built in 1780, which was also the first in a generation of cotton mills built to accommodate the spinning frames and carding engines invented and licenced by Richard Arkwright.

The location of such mills was determined by a requirement for close proximity to river courses providing water power to drive Arkwright's water frames and associated machinery. Numerous mills began to be constructed in rural Pennine areas along small and often isolated tributary valleys feeding into river courses.

Within the next 20 years over 30 mills had been constructed in the Worth Valley alone. By the early 1800s, over 200 new cotton mills were operational around the Calder Valley and to the west of Halifax, Bradford and Keighley. Cotton remained dominant in 1850 in locations such as Todmorden and Brighouse, which were important centres, as was the Craven district including Skipton.

In the Luddenden Valley ten separate mill operations (four worsted, three woollen, one cotton, one corn, one paper) were located along a 3.5-mile tributary stream running down from Cold Edge Dams to the valley floor, joining the River Calder at Luddenden Foot. In order to ensure a regular supply of water, the mill owners formed the Cold Edge Dam Company in the early 19th century, and by the 1830s the company maintained three large reservoirs high on the moors.[13]

Given that mills were built to accommodate similar sized machinery used by the differing textile industries, this resulted in a uniformity of building design. Between 1825 and 1875 mills grew rapidly in number and ever-increasing dimensions, although usually utilitarian in their design and construction.

The advent of steam power meant a transition away from water power, although some mills continued to use both to operate different types of machinery. Being no longer dependent on proximity to rivers and becks meant that mills could now be located in flatter valley floors, enabling both larger site footprints and close proximity to workforces in the growing cities and towns. Structural building advances also led to the introduction of cast iron columns, giving intermediate support to timber beams spanning the width of a mill, enabling buildings to be constructed with greater depth.

Fig 3.3 Loomshop, Chapel Lane, Addingham.

MACHELL BROS LIMITED.
ESTD 1856
SHODDY & MUNGO MANUFRS

MILL EMPLOYMENT

Although the focus of this book is on the physical building and architectural aspects of mills, it is important to consider the people who worked within them.

As an example, by 1833 Bents Mill employed 61 people, 42 of whom were under 14 years of age. All employees worked 69 hours per week – five 12-hour days with 9 hours on a Saturday. The following information was provided by the Bents Mill owners in response to a national survey undertaken by the North-Eastern District to Mill Owners and the Factory Commission.

It is fascinating to reflect on the mill owners' attitude to child labour, viewed through the lens of modern values and sensibilities. The following is the response of Richard Nichols and Co, owners of the neighbouring Hewenden Mill, in response to the Factory Commission's question regarding the hours of labour worked by children:

We disapprove entirely of legislative interference in commerce ... we oppose a restriction to any time less than 10 hours (per day) of labour of children ... that unless some absolute and positive provision be made for the instruction of children, their morals would not by any means be improved by a decrease in hours of labour, since their opportunity of associating with bad company would be increased; neither would their health be promoted, as especially in winter, they would expose themselves to the inclemency of the weather in insufficient clothing. ... the parents themselves are in a majority of cases ready to send their children to employment, from which the greatest wages may arise, often against the wishes of a Master; that children under nine years of age, are generally employed as a favour to parents, and at their special request; this may result from necessity or inconsideration on the part of the parents. That the temptation to intemperance, and means of its indulgence, contribute in the greatest degree to the improper ideas and conduct of the parents.

Answers of Messrs J W and W Knowles, Bents Mill, 1st May 1833 to queries:

	Males		**Females**	
	Numbers employed	*Average weekly wage*	*Numbers employed*	*Average weekly wage*
Under 10 years of age	5	1 shilling 11 pence	9	2 shillings 2 pence
10 and under 12 years	5	3 shillings 3 pence	7	3 shillings 10 pence
12 and under 14	5	4 shillings	11	4 shillings 8 pence
14 and under 16	–	–	2	6 shillings
16 and under 18	1	6 shillings 6 pence	5	6 shillings 9 pence
18 and under 21	–	–	3	6 shillings 9 pence
21 and upwards	2	8 shillings	6	7 shillings
	18		**43**	

Fig 3.4 Machell Brothers Mungo and Shoddy Mill, Dewsbury.

Lancashire mills

More than 2,400 mills and cloth-finishing works were built in the Greater Manchester conurbation, including many 'cotton towns' such as Bolton, Bury, Oldham, Rochdale, Salford, Stockport and Wigan. By the 1980s over half no longer existed, 'while many of the remainder were derelict or awaiting grant aided demolition'.[14]

The development of the canal network provided Manchester with transportation links to the port of Liverpool for the import of raw cotton and access to local coal, which became increasingly important due to the shift from water to steam power. In comparison to other regions, 'Manchester was distinguished by the number and scale of its early cotton mills, its dependence on steam power, its use of mills for spinning and the emphatically urban setting of its mills'.[15]

Manchester's only surviving 18th-century cotton mill is Old Mill, part of the 1789 section of Murrays' Mills. It originally comprised 8 storeys with 11 bays, with external engine house and boiler rooms attached to the east of the building. The mill was built in Ancoats, adjacent to the planned Rochdale canal, which opened in 1804 (**Fig 3.5**). As well as offering a transportation route, proximity to canals also provided a water supply for the steam engines, obviating the need to build reservoirs and enabling the clustering of mills in high-density configurations. Ancoats grew to become the world's first industrial suburb, with poor-quality back-to-back housing built close to the mills to accommodate immigrant workers arriving in Manchester.

Many early spinning mills comprised large multistorey buildings, usually six to eight storeys, with wings often subsequently attached at right angles. Most sites had an internal private yard which the major buildings faced on to. Entry into the courtyard would be via a covered passageway, or in larger mills, a lodge at the yard entrance.

In Lancashire, almost all later mills were constructed from red Accrington brick (**Fig 3.6**), whereas Yorkshire mills are mainly stone due to the availability of locally quarried millstone grit (although some in Leeds were built in brick). Lancashire mills tend to be built later – from the 1870s up to 1914 – and on the whole are much larger –

Fig 3.5 Murrays Mills, Ancoats, Manchester.

Fig 3.6 Butts Mill, Leigh.

BUTTS

Fig 3.8 Stonework at Salts Mill, Saltaire.

six or eight storeys rather than the four or five found to the east of the Pennines.[16] Architecturally, windows tend to be closer together, roofs often carry ornamental ironwork of roof balustrades, and there is a greater range in the design and detailing of mill chimneys, while use of white bricks to advertise the mill's name is much more prevalent compared to their Yorkshire counterparts.

There are few, if any, notable Lancashire architects associated with early mill developments, as cotton mills in the 1820s would be the combined product of a set of specialist trades such as millwrights, engineers and builders rather than being the design of one individual. However, by the late 19th century, specialist firms had begun to emerge, the most prolific architects being Abraham Stott and his brother Joseph Stott, whose rival businesses were commissioned to design many of the mills in Oldham and surrounding area.[17] Of particular concern for many mill owners was the frequent problem of fires given that mills contained combustible materials and timber beam spans which helped fires spread. The Stotts' emerging expertise in fireproofing building techniques gave them a distinct competitive advantage when tendering for mill commissions.

Mill architecture

The following is a list of architectural design features often found in mill buildings.

Italianate detailing was frequently applied to mill buildings in Yorkshire. Architects such as Lockwood and Mawson used such architectural treatments in the design of Salts Mill and the chimney in the New Mill, built in 1868, which they modelled on the campanile of the church of Santa Maria Gloriosa dei Frari in Venice (**Fig 3.7**). **Neo-Classical detailing** was more generally used on mills in parts of Lancashire, such as in Oldham, the most common

Fig 3.7 Chimney, New Mill, Saltaire.

Fig 3.9 Decorative columns and brick arches, Salts Mill.

Fig 3.10 Taking-in doors, Baildon Mills.

decorative elements being the use of pilasters with a stone cornice applied to the corners of a mill façade.[18]

The use of rustication – a masonry technique giving stone surfaces a rougher finish texture, contrasting with adjoining smooth blocks – became widely used. Rusticated window surrounds, doors and moulded cornices became more prevalent, adding detail and breaking the uniformity of bland elevations (**Fig 3.8**).[19]

The use of decorative elements such as double **pilasters**, stone mouldings, and dentilled or moulded **cornices** could be incorporated to highlight key features of mills, enabling owners to project an image of sophistication, wealth and success. However, the majority of mills were of much more basic utilitarian design.

Rows of **cast iron columns** gave intermediate support to timber beams, creating large open working spaces. Columns were almost always cast without any design, although in some instances, mills such as Salts Mill and Manningham Mills went to the expense of commissioning columns with 'decorative foliage capitals'.[20]

Fireproofing, such as the creation of brick arches supported by cast iron beams. Salts Mill was one of the first to incorporate this new technology (**Fig 3.9**).

External **towers** were incorporated to house staircases and toilets away from the main mill work floor. These often superseded privy towers in earlier mills which were, by necessity, located directly over water courses.

Taking-in doors were put in the upper floors of a mill through which materials could be winched from below. Later mills, for example Salts Mill, adjoined canals and had tiers of taking-in doors from which barges could be loaded and unloaded (**Fig 3.10**).

Weaving sheds were single-storey sheds built in the early to mid-19th century with distinctive saw-tooth roofs. Weaving sheds became prevalent due to the adoption of larger and heavier power looms. Working on one level made movement of long heavy rolls of woven cloth much easier, while the sheds were more suited to accommodating the vibrations and weight of power looms, avoiding potential structural damage in storeyed mills.

Good, even light was needed in order to eliminate shadows which may disguise faults in weaves. The north-facing saw-tooth angled roof windows provided even light across the whole shed, overcoming the restrictions when light was only available from side windows in multistorey mills.[21] Weaving sheds were invariably basic in design, without any architectural details. This, together with their extensive floorplate, has meant they are often demolished as part of mill development schemes (**Fig 3.11**).

Fig 3.11 Derelict weaving sheds, Dale End Mill.

Fig 3.12 Line shafts, Queens Street Mill, Burnley.

Fig 3.13 Iron feet brackets, Old Town Mill.

Fig 3.14 Building construction exhibit, Shrewsbury Flaxmill Maltings.

A **line shaft** is a power-driven rotating shaft which transmitted power from the steam engine to individual machines via leather belt drives. Storeyed mills would usually have a central line shaft running the whole length of each floor suspended from the beams by cast iron hangers (**Fig 3.12**).

Conventional timber trusses were used in the **roofs** of early mills, but as mills grew in size, trusses made of iron and, later, steel became used, often covering the mill in one span. To gain greater headroom, trusses were often raised up and sat on cast iron 'feet' brackets (**Fig 3.13**).

The iron **building frame** of Ditherington Flax Mill (now called Shrewsbury Flaxmill Maltings) was a pioneering engineering breakthrough. Rows of cast iron columns supported the beams, which in turn supported the arched brick ceiling. The structure was held together by metal nuts, bolts and wrought iron tie rods. The combination of iron columns, beams and wrought iron tie bars led to the development of stronger, lighter building frames, and ultimately shaped the design and construction of subsequent high-rise buildings (**Fig 3.14**).

To harness **water power**, where possible the mill would be situated on the bank of a small stream with water regulated by a dam and a bypass channel for when the mill was not operational. When it was not possible to locate the mill adjacent to the watercourse, a constructed channel would divert the flow of water to the mill.

Water power would be harnessed by constructing a mill-race above the mill which could often feed a dammed millpond, a wheel-race flowing past the mill and driving the waterwheel, and on to a tail-race leading back to the watercourse. Sometimes a millpond would be located below the mill to regulate the flow of water downstream.

The storing of water for later use by mill owners higher up the river and its impact on supply to mills downstream was a constant source of complaint, leading in some instances to legal proceedings. Drought would restrict water supply and thus power supplies, while flooding could raise the level of water in a mill tail-race and restrict the movement of the waterwheel.

The **waterwheel** was the sole source of power for the first generation of mills built adjacent to fast-flowing rivers and becks. River water was channelled from a river into a millpond and released during working hours to drive a waterwheel, located in a wheelhouse at the gable end of the mill. Water power continued to be used long after the invention of steam power, given its existing power generation capacity and the costs and difficulties of operating early steam engines.

WATERWHEEL AT DALE END MILL

Dale End Mill is a Grade II* listed mill located close to the Pennine Way at Lothersdale. In 1792 Thomas Parker converted the mill from corn-grinding to textile manufacturing and by 1835 the mill was given over to worsted spinning. The subsequent expansion of the mill, including the addition of weaving sheds in the 1850s, created the need for a larger waterwheel supplemented by a steam engine and the addition of a 90ft chimney.

In 1852 James Ellison designed and built the magnificent 45ft-diameter suspension wheel. The wheel at Dale End Mill is reputed to be the largest indoor waterwheel in the world and a superb example of the millwright's craft. The waterwheel and steam engine together provided the power for 190 looms and 1,700 spindles. The waterwheel was powered via a mill pond in the village with water flowing through a goit (a narrow channel) and linking to the beck which runs directly under the mill.

Waterwheel, Dale End Mill.

A **steam power** plant consisted of three elements: an engine house, boiler house and a chimney. A later addition was often an Economiser (*see* p. 50). Engine houses were usually tall buildings needed to accommodate the height and movement of a beam engine and fly wheel. Engine houses could often span three storeys. The transition from beam to horizontal engines often necessitated building alterations to create a longer and narrower building.

Engine houses were often showcases for engineering technological innovations (**Fig 3.15**). Consequently, in larger mills engine houses were often given ornamental treatments with large arched windows, wood panelled boarded rooms, decorative floor tiles and, in some cases, carved friezes and panels. Conversely, boiler houses were

Fig 3.15 The Engine House, Shipley.

of basic utilitarian design with little or no architectural detailing. Engine houses would be positioned to the side of early mills, although often located in more central locations in later mills. In order to avoid explosions or fire risks to the main mill, the boiler would be attached to the engine house, which in turn would be located adjacent or within the mill to avoid a direct connection between boiler and mill.

The introduction of steam engines was transformational, as mills were no longer reliant on watercourses as a power source and could now be built on flat valley floor sites with land available for expansion, improved access to the rail and canal networks, and closer proximity to urban workforces (**Fig 3.16**).

Fig 3.16 Canal network, Five Rise locks, Bingley.

The **Green's Economiser,** designed by Edward Green, made savings by extracting the exhaust gases from the boiler furnace to heat boiler feed water, pumped through a series of pipes, thereby reducing the energy needed to produce steam. Publicity for the Economiser made claims of saving 'between 15 to 25% in coal'. The remains of a Green's Economiser can be seen at Dale End Mill in Lothersdale, one of the few still in existence. Stacks of metal pipes arranged in the flues leading from the boiler to the chimney can be seen in **Fig 3.17**.

The **mill chimney** has become an iconic image symbolising the northern industrial landscape. The chimney had two purposes – to disperse boiler furnace exhaust fumes and to create a down draught to assist in the working of the furnaces. 'Both functions were affected by the height of the chimney, greater powers of dispersal and draught being derived from taller chimneys than from small.'[22] For obvious reasons, mill chimneys were situated as close to boiler houses as possible.

The most common type of chimney before the 1820s was of square design tapering towards the top. From this date onwards, chimneys became higher as power demand and output increased, and evolved to more tapered octagonal cross-section profiles. Often the height and location of the chimney were used by mill owners as symbols of prestige and self-promotion. In Lancashire, and more occasionally Yorkshire, the prominence of chimneys was used as advertising, with the mill names articulated in white brickwork to the top of the parapet, tower or chimney (**Fig 3.18**).

Mill chimneys were often given decorative treatments such as the Lister Mills chimney, built in Bradford for the Manningham works of Lister & Co. The chimney is a monumental structure dominating the Bradford skyline and visible for miles. Both the chimney and mill were designed by local architects Andrews and Pepper. Construction took two years and on completion in 1873 it stood 250 feet high and 22 feet square at its base. As was the case with Salts Mill, the architects used Italianate decorative elements; the chimney design was based on the Campanile in Venice and incorporates two elaborate cornices, one at 190 feet and one on the top of the structure (**Fig 3.19**).

Fig 3.17 Green's Economiser, Dale End Mill.

Where mills were located at the bottom of steep valleys, often a chimney might be located further up the hillside, linked to the boiler house by an underground flue. In many cases the original mills are no longer in existence, but the chimneys remain, leading to the somewhat surreal

Fig 3.18 Chimney, Queen Street Mill, Burnley.

Fig 3.19 Lister Mills chimney, Bradford.

Fig 3.20 Chimney Meadow, Harden, Bingley.

sight of an isolated chimney in the middle of open fields with no apparent reason for its existence (**Fig 3.20**).

Following the decline of the textile industry, mill chimneys were regarded as obsolete structures which could not be adapted to other uses while being costly and difficult to maintain (**Fig 3.21**). Consequently, demolition was seen as the only solution. Fred Dibnah, the 1970s TV celebrity steeplejack, learnt his trade maintaining chimneys, only to realise there was lucrative work in felling them. Rather than using explosives, he devised a method of cutting a hole in the base of the chimney which would be supported by wooden props. The props would be burnt so that the chimney would eventually topple. The TV audience's attention would be gripped by waiting to see if our Fred could get the chimney to fall in its intended direction. By the end of his life Dibnah had demolished 90 chimneys.[23]

Increasingly chimneys have been retained, often as part of planning consents. A small number have also found second uses as makeshift telecoms towers.

Development of mill complexes

Even in the 1770s the textile industry had begun to divide into distinct subsectors. In the case of Yorkshire, these were wool, worsted, flax and linen. Cotton production was added in the late 18th century, silk manufacture to a lesser degree and carpet manufacture by the 19th and mid-19th century respectively. The dominant industry by far became the woollen sector, and by the end of the 19th century 925 woollen mills represented 44% of all textile establishments.[24]

From 1825 onwards, a number of mills began to incorporate additional buildings involved in the process of turning raw material into finished cloth products. Prior to this, the separate stages of cloth production such as

Fig 3.21 Dean Clough millscape.

Fig 3.22 Oats Royd Mill.

spinning, weaving and dyeing had been undertaken by different businesses at their own premises. Integrated woollen mill complexes began to appear where manufacturers, with access to new forms of investment capital, would bring all the various production stages 'in house' to reduce costs and exert greater control. This was a significant change from the previous arrangement of contracting out the respective processing activities to smaller manufacturers.

Consequently, the sites of integrated woollen mills began to evolve to house a range of buildings grouped around the original multistoreyed mill such as weaving sheds, dyehouses, dryhouses, engine room, chimney, offices, warehouses, workshops, yard and stables etc. The respective buildings were situated according to their need for close proximity to the mill's power source – either engine house or waterwheel chamber. They were also clustered together according to their role in the production process and to minimise the time taken in transporting materials around the site. However, it would be wrong to suggest that site building configurations adhered to any overall long-term master plans. Rather, mills tended to evolve piecemeal over time, leading to large sprawling sites.

By 1870 in Yorkshire, integrated mills were the commonest method of production. The growing dominance of integrated woollen mills also brought an end to any form of outworking, replaced by the establishment of waged workforces directly employed by the mill owner. It can therefore be argued that the early integrated woollen mills of the 19th century were the precursor to modern-day integrated manufacturing factory complexes (**Fig 3.22**).

It is important to acknowledge the scale of machinery technology innovations and entrepreneurialism which drove the evolution of integrated mill complexes. This was only achieved by leading mill owners taking significant risks to invest in new machinery prototypes. Samuel Cunliffe Lister (1851–1906), the creator and owner of Manningham Mills, is reported to have had seven different textile machine prototypes at various stages of construction in his nine separate mills. During his lifetime he spent £600,000 on 'working out new ideas', a sum so vast it brought him close to bankruptcy on several occasions.[25]

Historic growth of the textile sector

It is hard to comprehend the extent to which mills grew in number and scale. It is estimated that over 2,000 textile mills were built in Yorkshire alone between 1770 and 1930. In 1874 there were 998 woollen mills employing 76,800 people, while there were 520 worsted mills employing a total of 114,300.[26]

A further development was that of local area specialisations as different towns and cities diversified into one specific textile industry subsector or product type. In the case of Yorkshire, narrow cloths were made in and around Huddersfield, white cloth and blankets around Dewsbury, coloured cloths to the north and east of Leeds, and worsted production was concentrated around Bradford in the Worth and Upper Aire Valley, around Keighley and along the Calder Valley. Mungo and shoddy, the process by which woollen rags were recycled to create raw materials for new products, became dominant in areas of West Yorkshire such as Batley, Dewsbury, Osset and Morley.

This diverse range of specialism can be regarded as being complementary rather than competitive, given that they provided work for a wide range of local specialists who formed an integrated supply chain network.

Millscapes

Mills were the original 'place-makers' shaping the localities that developed around them.

SALTS MILL

Salts Mill is perhaps the finest example of a purpose-built integrated mill complex. Built between 1850 and 1853 for Titus Salt, on completion Salts Mill was the largest building (55,000 sq yd) in the world. Henry Lockwood and William Mawson were successful local architects who had undertaken previous commissions for Titus Salt, but had never worked on industrial or manufacturing buildings prior to their appointment to design Salts Mill. It is also important to recognise the contribution of Sir William Fairburn, the contracted engineer, who was responsible for designing the power transmission and introducing innovative fireproofing techniques at the mill.

When complete, the mill spanned 11.5 acres, with two steam engines driving 1,200 looms, which, at the time, was almost double the number of the largest local mill. Built at a cost of £100,000, at its peak Salts Mill employed 3,200 people and produced 18 miles of cloth per day.[59]

Lockwood and Mawson clearly worked closely with Titus Salt in designing a coherent arrangement of linked buildings geared to maximising the efficiency of worsted manufacturing. The spine of the building was a large five-storey warehouse, 25 bays long, with direct access onto the Leeds and Liverpool Canal. Wool deliveries would arrive by canal barge and be sorted prior to being transported to the adjacent combing shed where it would be washed, dried and combed. On the eastern side of the warehouses was a vast weaving shed. Both the weaving and combing sheds had north-facing roof windows. The main mill was attached at a right angle to the southern end of the warehouses, creating a public-facing façade fronting the railway line. Offices were located on the western perimeter of the site along what became Victoria Road. The southern elevation also contained two steam engine houses linked to an underground boiler house and a 68m-tall chimney.

In 1871 the New Mill was constructed on the opposite side of the canal to undertake textile dyeing, which had previously been contracted out to local suppliers.

Apart from the sheer scale of the mill complex, what is remarkable is the range of building innovations incorporated in Salts Mill, including

- The standard bay size was considerably enlarged by the adoption of fireproofing construction methods involving the use of hollow bricks to improve ventilation and reduce the weight of arched ceilings.

Salts Mill.

Far left Salts Mill roof gallery.

Left Jonathan Silver and former assistant Alan South working on the 1853 Hockney Gallery.

Courtesy of Bradford Telegraph *and* Argus, *Newquest Media Group*

- The roofing structure was particularly advanced, using a system of cast iron struts and wrought iron rods which, unlike the floors below, did not require cast iron columns for support. Cast iron trusses were expensive to produce and expanded when heated, putting pressure on external walls. A solution was developed using both wrought iron rods for tension and cast iron struts for compression. The result was a huge undivided space which was 'considered to be the single largest room in the world at the time'.[60]

- The roof of the warehouse contained a 70,000-gallon iron water tank, showing the phenomenal strength of the building. Rainwater recycling was undertaken by storing rain, collected from the mill roofs, into a half million-gallon storage reservoir situated beneath the weaving shed.

- The boiler house was situated underground, enabling coal to be tipped directly into it from the adjacent railway siding.

- The drive shafts were hidden within the floor structure to reduce the risk of industrial injuries. Floors were connected via specially designed recesses in the brick-vaulted ceilings.

Lockwood and Mawson frequently used Italianate-inspired architectural treatments in many of their previous commissions, such as Bradford City Hall, and applied these, albeit sparingly, to Salts Mill. The chimney in the New Mill was based on the campanile of the Church of Santa Maria Gloriosa dei Frari in Venice. In terms of architectural details, 'the multi-storey mill has rusticated pilasters, voussoired arches, different window forms and an overall moulded cornice, as well as a more elaborated centrepiece surmounted by pavilion towers'.[61]

Salts Mill inspired greater ornamentation in mill architecture, with mill owners keen to promote their wealth and prestige via more elaborate mill complex designs.

Recent transformation

Salts Mill passed through many owners until production finally ended in the early 1980s and the mill lay empty.

Jonathan Silver was a Bradford-born, local entrepreneur who had created a number of successful businesses spanning menswear, antiques and art. Silver had been in a previous joint venture with Ernest Hall, acquiring and regenerating the Dean Clough Mill complex in Halifax. In 1987 he succeeded in buying Salts Mill at Saltaire from the then current owner Illingworth Morris.

Dean Clough provided Silver with a test bed for many ideas he would later bring to Salts Mill. Silver had created and run a successful bar called Crossleys and gained valuable experience, including the marketing and letting of space at Dean Clough. The business relationship became strained by the two partners' differing styles and approaches. Hall bought out Silver's share of the business in 1984, although they remained firm friends.

Having the idea of creating an art gallery at Salts Mill, Jonathan Silver persuaded acquaintance David Hockney to lend some of his pictures to establish the 1853 Gallery. Silver was a hands-on manager and was personally involved in much of the renovation works such as stripping back the existing cream and blue paint on the mill walls to reveal superb stonework.

Silver has been described as a showman with enormous creative energy who developed a succession of high-quality free arts exhibitions and events which generated local and national publicity, gradually altering the perception of Salts Mill and Saltaire as desirable places to live and work. Salts Mill has subsequently grown to accommodate further galleries, a book shop, diner, independent retailers, exhibition areas and extensive workspace for a wide range of tenant businesses. The importance of Salts Mill, together with Dean Clough, cannot be overestimated – they were both trailblazers demonstrating how vast mill complexes could be successfully repurposed for uses that were previously unimaginable and became role models for many subsequent mill renovation projects.

Silver was an enigmatic, energetic and demanding visionary who had a gift for making things happen. Jonathan Silver died of cancer in 1997 at the age of just 47. Salts Mill continues to be operated by members of the Silver family.

The rapid expansion of the textile sector during the Industrial Revolution led to a change in the settlement patterns of many rural villages. In the case of Addingham, in West Yorkshire, the small village originally functioned as a traditional farming community with a dispersed pattern of farms and agricultural buildings. However, in the late 18th century the advent of the textile sector led, over a 50-year period, to a population increase from around 500 to 2,000 villagers. In physical development terms, this involved the construction of handweavers' cottages, loomshops and five mills infilling land between the existing farms, resulting in Addingham developing the nucleated settlement pattern we recognise today. The last working textile mills closed in the 1970s, although Low Mill had an extended life of wool processing between 1999 and 2006.

In cities the urbanisation process was much more profound and widespread. The area of Ancoats in Manchester has been described as the world's first industrial suburb. The first mills were built in Ancoats as early as 1790, and rapid industrial expansion resulted in numerous mills, workshops and factories being constructed in the area. Arable farmland, adjacent to the industrial areas, was developed to create a grid pattern of back-to-back houses to accommodate new arrivals attracted by the availability of employment. By 1851 Ancoats' population exceeded 50,000 and was larger than many local towns. Squalid, cramped and unsanitary conditions soon led to the creation of Manchester's first slum, described by Engels 'as a densely populated and unlovely tract'.[27]

This process was replicated throughout the north of England with the building of mills followed by the construction of surrounding streets of terrace houses to accommodate the new urban working class (**Fig 3.23**). The resulting wide-scale urbanisation of northern towns

Fig 3.23 Skipton millscape.

and cities led to unimaginable population growth. Between 1821 and 1831 the populations of Salford and Manchester grew by 47% and Bradford by a staggering 78%.[28]

Model villages

The appalling conditions in urban suburbs led to a small number of mill owners building houses and amenities to improve conditions for their workforces. Motivated by a mixture of Christian values, social determinism and enlightened self-interest, mill owners such as James and Edward Akroyd and Titus Salt bought areas of land to create new communities or 'model villages' to improve the living conditions of their workforce:

> *The houses were created not merely with the purpose of aggregating a sufficient number of operatives for the supply of labour but also with an eye to the improvement of their social conditions, fitting up their homes with every requisite comfort and convenience.*
>
> Colonel Edward Akroyd

Copley was the first model village built by a 'millocrat' – Edward Akroyd – and was constructed between 1847 and 1853. The village contained 112 houses built around the mill, and amenities included a library, Sunday school, allotments, church, and workers' canteen. Edward Akroyd subsequently commissioned George Gilbert Scott to design a second village in the Bankfield area of Halifax. The resultant model village, Akroydon, built between 1855 and 1876, contained not only high-quality housing, built in a Gothic style, but also other village amenities including a church, cemetery, village green, allotments and a co-operative shop. Housing was allocated on a hierarchical basis according to skills and status, and workers were given the opportunity to purchase and own their homes through a 15-year loan arrangement through the Akroydon Building Association (**Fig 3.24**).[29]

Saltaire

However, neither Copley nor Akroydon were on the same scale as Saltaire, constructed west of Salts Mill on the banks of the Aire near Bradford. Titus Salt commissioned architects Lockwood and Mawson to design a village on a 25-acre site adjacent to the mill to provide housing and amenities for his workforce. Work began on constructing Saltaire in 1851. By 1871, 824 houses, 40 shops and 45 almshouses had been built, housing 4,300 workers.

The village was constructed on a grid pattern with the main public buildings assembled along Victoria Street, the main route to the mill. Architectural styling followed that of the mill, with the use of Italianate detailing. Houses were for rent and not sale, as in Akroydon, and were graded by style (**Fig 3.25**).

Fig 3.24 Akroydon model village.

Fig 3.25 Saltaire model village.

MILLS AND SUSTAINABILITY

In many cases mills pioneered the use of 'green' design features, although clearly the motivation of mill owners was to reduce costs rather than any commitment to environmentalism.

Early water-driven mills harnessed renewable energy for their power source, although water supplies could be intermittent in times of drought and when a number of upstream mills were competing to utilise the river course.

Rainwater harvesting was pioneered at Salts Mill. Rainwater recycling was undertaken by storing rain, collected from the mill roofs, into a half million-gallon storage reservoir situated beneath the weaving shed. The roof of the warehouse also contained an additional 70,000-gallon water tank.

Old Town Mill near Hebden Bridge was one of the first mills in the area to have access to hydro-electricity. This was generated by a river turbine at the bottom of the valley, with the power being fed through cables up the hillside to the mill. Similarly, at Hebden Bridge Mill, during the 1950s, clothing manufacturers Greenwood and Pickles attached a generator to the mill waterwheel to power their machines, and eventually to supply electric lighting. Greenwood and Pickles finally closed in 1956 and parts of the mill fell into disrepair. In 1973 David Fletcher, a local businessman and environmentalist, rescued the derelict mill which was about to be demolished to create car parking. Fletcher installed a new wheel and Archimedes screw and Hebden Bridge Mill now generates power through means of a modern turbine and heat transfer pump.

Dewsbury has been described as 'the greenest town in England'[62] due to its 19th-century role as an international recycling centre for woollen cloth. The town specialised in the production of 'shoddy' and 'mungo' – heavy cloth made from recycled rags often used to make soldiers' great coats and blankets. The growing affluence of Dewsbury led to the construction of three separate stations to service the volume of cloth transported to the town for processing and a series of architecturally outstanding warehouses designed in an Italian Renaissance Revival style.

Temple Works in Leeds was also the first building to incorporate a green roof. Built between 1838 and 1841 for the Marshall family, the flax mill was designed to be an integrated mill bringing together weaving and spinning in a single-storey layout. To increase natural light, 66 conical glass skylights were installed across a single room in which, at its height, were employed 2,600 workers.

In 1843 John Marshall added a remarkable office building whose façade incorporated architectural features modelled on those of several Egyptian temples. The original chimney was inspired by Cleopatra's Needle, but was replaced in 1852 with a more conventional design when it became unstable.

Once the main building became operational, it was found that the lack of humidity in the mill caused the linen thread to dry quickly and fibres to break. It was decided this problem could be tackled by laying a green roof. Having installed the turf roof it was decided that the problem of ongoing maintenance would be solved by a herd of sheep grazing on the roof grass. However, it was then discovered that sheep are unable to climb stairs. To overcome this problem, the first ever hydraulic lift was created to transport the sheep to the roof level.[63]

Surprisingly few mills have installed solar panels to reduce energy costs, especially as the pitch of many existing mill roofs would lend itself to solar arrays. However, Lister Mills has recently secured planning permission to install a series of solar panels, given they will not alter the mill's historic roofline and visual appearance.

Current-day mill developers are becoming increasingly aware of the embodied carbon in buildings and the cost implications of disposing of waste building materials. In the case of the Old Town Mill near Hebden Bridge scheme, all surplus stone generated by the redevelopment is reused, for example in the creation of new dry-stone walls, with no stone removed from the site.

Temple Works, Leeds.

Fig 3.26 Corporation Mill, Sowerby Bridge.

Overlockers were allocated the best houses, complete with sitting room, kitchen, scullery, cellar and three bedrooms. Public amenities in Saltaire included a church, hospital, alms houses, railway station, school, wash house, library, shops, concert hall, billiards room, science laboratory and park. However, there were no licenced premises in the village.

Industrial hinterlands

Mill operations also created business opportunities and employment in ancillary industries, shaping the development of adjoining urban areas. According to Goddard and Gray,[30] the mills in Sowerby supported 'tanneries (to produce leather belt drives for machinery), iron works and manufacturers of steam engines, brass foundries, stone quarries, bobbin works and wire-making works – used in carding machines to prepare wool for spinning, as well as in looms' (**Fig 3.26**).

The growth of supply chain industries located close to mills created industrial hinterlands and the further growth of urban areas. Many local engineering companies, originally set up to supply mills, evolved to assume dominant roles in the local economy. In fact, such firms often continued to grow and became major local employers long after the decline of the textile industries which first helped to foster them.

The decline of the textile industry

In 1970, approximately 1,142,000 people were employed in the textile and clothing industries in the UK. By 1991, the figure was 347,000.[31] In Yorkshire alone, more than 300 mills closed between 1950 and 1967.

To consider the impact on just one city, in Bradford in 1950 there were still 1,123 wool and worsted mills operating in the city. By 2008 the figure was only four. Between 1979 and 1981, 16,000 textile and engineering workers in Bradford lost their jobs.[32]

Trade barriers, growing foreign competition, removal of import duties and the introduction of synthetic materials all contributed to a gradual decline in the northern textile sector. A further factor was a move away from formal attire to more casual dress, including, according to Gary Firth, 'increased demand for lighter clothing as a result of the introduction of domestic central heating and car heaters'.[33] Labour shortages in the 1950s meant that mill owners had to compete for workers with other newer industries that offered better pay and conditions. To attract local labour, mills had to increase wages, resulting in a downward spiral, with the UK textile manufacturers becoming increasingly less competitive than their foreign counterparts.

The industry also suffered from an image problem, with parents discouraging their offspring from entering into mill employment. In the words of a teenager interviewed for BBC Regional News in 1957, 'The cotton industry's future is uncertain. I've also been influenced by my parents. My Mum was a weaver for some time and she impressed on me that conditions are bad and wages are poor'.[34]

Many mills became abandoned and were soon plundered for any metals or valuables that could be easily transported. Mill owners found they were unable to sell their properties but still had to pay vacant building rates. Many decided to cut their losses and demolish their mills and sell the salvaged stone and slate. What saved mills in many cases was their sheer scale and the effort and costs involved in their demolition. Photographer Peter Mitchell, who has spent his life documenting Leeds, argues that the city has suffered far more in the way of demolition and clearance because its buildings, such as mills, were built of brick, whereas neighbouring areas of West Yorkshire were constructed in stone and therefore were much harder to demolish.

MILLS AND MIGRANT WORKERS

Mills have played a significant role in determining the ethnic composition of towns and cities across the north of England.

In the case of Bradford, the Irish Famine of 1845 led to an influx of immigrants, and by 1851 the Irish made up 10% of the city's population. The new migrants worked mainly in the declining trades of hand-weaving and hand-combing and were resented by local people for being Gaelic speakers and for their Roman Catholicism.[64] A further group of more affluent migrants were from Europe – mainly northern Germany. This cohort of well-educated and cosmopolitan merchants played a significant role in the commercial, civic and cultural life of Bradford and were responsible for founding the Bradford Chamber of Commerce and sponsoring the St George's Hall concert venue. The composer Frederick Delius was born in Bradford to a prosperous mercantile German family.

Little Germany, a district within the city, is the legacy of mainly German merchants who from 1855 onwards invested significant sums in building architecturally distinctive warehouses and offices for the storage and sale of export goods.

Although a small number of often Jewish settlers arrived from Russia, Poland, Austria and Germany during the inter-war period, it was only after the Second World War that overseas workers arrived in significant numbers. Many civilians displaced by the war arrived in Bradford. Ukrainian refugees formed the largest Ukrainian community in Europe, drawn to the city by the availability of employment in the textile industries. The European Volunteer Workers settlement programme also led to hundreds of women from southern Italy arriving in Bradford, directly recruited by large textile employers.[65]

During the 1950s and 1960s the textile industry, in the face of increasing foreign competition, began to invest in new machinery and moved to three-shift 24-hour working patterns. Women were prevented by UK law from working night shifts, and in a buoyant labour market it proved difficult to find

Little Germany, Bradford.

local men prepared to work night shifts. Following such labour shortages, textile mills actively recruited first from Eastern Europe and the West Indies and after 1955 from Pakistan and India.

Asian men were employed to fill gaps in the shift pattern and were encouraged by mill owners to recruit others from their extended family networks. Word of mouth about the availability of jobs led to increasing numbers of immigrants arriving in Bradford and other parts of West Yorkshire. In the case of Bradford, Hindus and Sikhs came first to the city from the Punjab and Gujarat, with small numbers arriving in the late 1950s. Pakistan Muslims arrived in greater numbers, and by 1964 Bradford had a population of 12,000 Pakistanis. Many recruits were paid wages half that of the average indigenous worker.[66]

In the words of one Asian worker,[67]

"Well, if you can go back to the 1950s, there was a boom, especially in textiles and they couldn't find enough people to run the mills, so getting a job were no problem ... In the department where my father worked, 80% of the people were Asian and they were the ones that did the jobs such as spinning, which were the dirty, or the hard jobs ... I remember we used to get mill owners coming and knocking on our doors to say "Have you got any labour or anything".

The Asian migrants were young men usually in their twenties who came to earn money to support their families back home. Initially the men lived in cheap-rent multi-occupancy housing in inner-city areas and viewed their stay in the UK as temporary.

In 1962 the announcement of the Commonwealth Immigration Act, restricting migration from the Commonwealth to Britain, encouraged migrant workers to settle in Bradford and send for their families before the act became law. Self-contained communities began to emerge which newcomers could join to be among others with a shared identity, language and religion and in close proximity to places of worship, food shops, employment and community meeting places.

Patterns of immigrant settlement began to develop in specific wards within urban areas – as an example, in the area of Manningham, Bradford, the former mill owners' and managers' large houses with multiple rooms became increasingly sought after given they were suited to the Asian pattern of living among extended family networks.

Wide-scale immigration, generated in part by the availability of mill employment, has had a profound impact on the ethnic composition of communities across northern towns and cities. According to William Gaunt of Sunny Bank Mills, 'West Yorkshire has welcomed folk from across the globe, as they sought work in mills and put down roots here, bringing their culture and food with them. Now these families are a central part of the community and our identity'.[68]

Worker at Daniel Illingworth Mill, Bradford.
Courtesy of Bradford Museums Photo Archive

The Carding Shed (Washpit Mills)

The Carding Shed is home to IK Sport Classic and the Oil Can Café – two unique businesses established by Ian and Nicola Kellet. The Carding Shed is part of the former 200-year-old Washpit woollen mill complex located in the Holme Valley near Holmfirth.

IK Sport Classic provides a complete range of car restoration services to UK and international collectors, including engine rebuilds, a body shop, parts manufacture, paint spraying, and servicing. Currently there are 90 classic cars, some dating back to the 1930s, being worked on or stored for collectors at the Carding Shed.

The Oil Can Café is home to an eclectic mix of motoring and cycling ephemera and has become a destination attraction with regular clientele, as well as bookings for its events space. The café takes its inspiration from the Goodwood Revival Festival and has grown to a point where it serves 1,000–1,200 meals a week. Nicola also ran a vintage clothing business from the mill, but has since closed this to concentrate on the café. Both businesses jointly provide employment for 30 local people.

Ian originally set up and ran his own business at Dobroyd Mill in Hepworth, but as the lease neared expiry, Ian and Nicola began the search for a new location. Finding an alternative mill was an important consideration as it was felt that a traditional mill environment was in keeping with the theme of classic and vintage cars. The Carding Shed, part of Washpit

Above Nicola Kellet.

Left Ian Kellet.

Opposite Classic car display.

SHELL
JKH 980L

THE
OIL CAN CAFÉ
AT THE CARDING SHED
UK CLASSICS
GARAGE SERVICES
AT
THE
CARDING SHED
HOLMFIRTH

Above and right Oil Can Café.

Opposite The Carding Shed.

Mills, became available; however, substantial work was needed to update the run-down mill, including extensive partitioning to create separate workshops, building the bakery and filling large pits under the Carding Shed floor with polystyrene blocks before concreting over. The building was finally finished in May 2018 and both businesses collectively occupy approximately 40,000 sq ft at Washpit Mills.

The couple live on site in a flat located within the mill and have a strong bond with the building. According to Ian, 'The first time we walked into the mill we had the feeling that it was saying "thank goodness", I'm now going to have something going on that I'll enjoy ... It's a whacking great mill and it's the best thing ever ... It's very welcoming and protective.'[54]

Woodhouse Mill

Woodhouse Mill in Todmorden was badly fire-damaged in the 1990s and had no roof and a collapsed gable wall, while the three remaining walls were slowly falling into the adjoining Rochdale Canal. The Grade II listed, five-storey mill, built in 1832, was on the Heritage at Risk Register.

Charles Moran left school aged 15 without any qualifications and became a panel beater. He subsequently became the founder and managing director of the world's fourth largest demolition company, the Yorkshire-based Controlled Demolition Group. Following the sale of the business, Charles decided that rather than 'knock things down' he would turn his attentions instead to restoring a local eye-sore mill. Charles purchased Woodhouse Mill in 2001 for around £30,000 and set about turning it into 20 contemporary apartments. Using local labour, Moran employed a team of 30 men on site, including 6 stonemasons who repaired cracked lintels and restored other original features.

Charles Moran.

Initially, an extensive steel girder framework needed to be assembled inside the building to reinforce the remaining structure, together with 50 concrete supports for added strength. A series of external 'bulls-eye' wall anchor plates tie the walls to the steel skeleton. Extensive work needed to be undertaken to strengthen the foundations, while original architectural features such as cast iron pillars were retained within the building. Special attention had also to be paid to acoustic dampening to stop noise transfer between apartments.

The mill was fully restored by 2002.

Before and after.

Old Town Mill

Old Town Mill, or Mitchell Mill as it is known locally, is a Grade II listed former textile mill situated at Pecket Well, north of Hebden Bridge. The mill is a prominent landmark on the horizon with stunning views towards Heptonstall and Stoodley Pike. The mill dates back to 1851 with later additions in the 1880s. The mill was extended in the 1890s for the Mitchell Brothers to accommodate a worsted mill and canteen block. Around 1895 a further phase of development began with plans to create a new reservoir above the mill. In the early 1960s the mill was sold and the buildings were turned over to poultry keeping, sheepskin rug manufacture and cattle.

Old Town Mill is a good example of an integrated mill where an original weaving shed becomes adapted to incorporate advancements in mechanisation – for example the addition of the engine room for a small beam engine.

The mill was acquired by Clay Developments, a family-owned business based in Huddersfield. It is now being restored to provide 21 new homes and business units. The scheme, designed by Gayle Appleyard of Gagarin Studio, involves the conversion of the buildings to provide townhouses inspired by the local vernacular of Hebden's 'double-decker'

Left Ben Clay.

Below Mill gates.

Old Town – Michell Mill.

Townhouses.

Before and after.

over-and-under dwellings. The chimney will remain as an independent structure set in landscaping incorporating the former millpond. The first phase saw the creation of four new-build townhouses on part of the site, followed by the second phase of converting the main mill building into apartments.

Ben Clay is clearly passionate about restoring the building and is leading a small team of skilled craftsmen who are painstakingly restoring the mill to accommodate new uses while retaining historic features within this landmark building.

CASE STUDY

Bents Mill

Bents Mill, near Cullingworth, was originally constructed in 1799 for the purposes of cotton spinning. The three-storey building is a fairly typical mill design and construction utilising locally quarried stone, uniform fenestration, internal staircases set in their own compartments, and taking-in doors. The curved 'privy' tower, which provided toilet facilities for the workers, was deemed to be of exceptional architectural interest and was one of the reasons the mill was awarded a Grade II listing.[55]

By 1833 it employed 61 people, 42 of whom were under the age of 14. The mill stood empty and derelict for 15 years prior to its purchase in 1997 by Janet and John Emanuel. In 1977 the Emanuels had previously bought and restored nearby Hewenden Mill.

Bents Mill's roof had to be stripped and replaced, the chimney rebuilt, extensive groundworks undertaken, the road leading into the mill improved and a vast rockery constructed to keep the steep slope stable. A road was forged through the wood connecting Bents Mill with Hewenden Mill and the ponds were reinstated.

The renovation of Bents Mill was completed in 2004 and now provides holiday apartment accommodation (*see* also Fig. 4.2, p. 90).

Winter at Bents Mill.

Before ...

Courtesy of Susan Emmanuel

After ...

Crusader Works

Crane reflection.

Crusader Works in Manchester was built in the late 1840s by George Parr, Matthew Curtis and William Madeley and is a rare example of a large, mid-19th-century textile machinery works. Known originally as the Phoenix Works, the huge new factory included an iron foundry built on the opposite side of Chapeltown Street. It was among the earliest and largest purpose-built textile machinery works in Manchester.

In 1894, the works were acquired by John Hetherington & Sons, another leading manufacturer of textile machinery. Hetherington & Sons continued to produce machinery at Crusader Works until the early 1920s.

The building was awarded a Grade II listing in 1994. Capital & Centric acquired the building in 2017 when it was semi-derelict, and embarked on a sympathetic residential conversion creating 123 apartments together with a community courtyard and other amenities.

Mill schemes such as Crusader Works have been a catalyst in driving investment and regeneration in major city centres such as Manchester. Creating a residential community with a shared courtyard has brought new life to an area now called Piccadilly East. Many additional apartment blocks are under construction as illustrated by the number of cranes in the area.

Corridor.

TRAMWAY
LOOK BOTH
WAYS

Crusader Works.

4

Mill regeneration: Policy approaches

New uses for old mills

There is a misconception that the repurposing of mills first began in the 1980s with the likes of Dean Clough and Salts Mill. In fact, new and varied uses have been found for mills throughout their lifespan; for example, as early as the 1870s old multistorey mills in Halifax were being converted by Mackintosh for the making of confectionary.

In rural areas mills were sometimes repurposed as entertainment venues providing leisure attractions for day visitors from local towns and cities. Goit Stock Mill, near Cullingworth, was converted in 1919 to the 'Happy Valley Pleasure Grounds', with a ballroom located on the upper floor of the mill. The mill also had a café able to accommodate up to 1,500 people, while attractions within its grounds included boating on the mill pond, roundabouts, a monkey house, putting greens, a woodland toboggan run and walks to the picturesque Goit Stock waterfall. At its height the mill attracted up to 20,000 day visitors arriving at Bingley and Cullingworth railway stations and transported by charabanc to the Pleasure Grounds. In 1927 the mill burnt to the ground, and despite attempts to relaunch Happy Valley the attraction finally closed in 1932. The site has since been redeveloped as a caravan park and all that now remains of the mill is a lone chimney on the hillside meadow

Similarly, Gibson Mill near Hebden Bridge (**Fig 4.1**) was a cotton mill throughout the 19th century before it was closed and later converted in the early 1900s to an 'entertainment emporium for the public'. The facilities included 'dining saloons, a dance hall, a roller-skating rink, refreshment kiosks and boating on the mill pond'.[35]

Understandably, following the rapid decline of the textile industries in the 1970s–1980s, the focus of local and national politicians was on the human costs of wide-scale unemployment rather than on the problem of vast areas of vacant industrial property.

Fig 4.1 Gibson Mill, Hebden Bridge.

A report produced by SAVE Britain's Heritage in 1979 argued passionately for the retention of mill buildings as part of the nation's industrial heritage. SAVE's research found that few, if any, local authorities had specific planning or economic development policies for mills and viewed each scheme on its merits[36] – in fact, a similar situation to the present day. The research project argued for a mill inventory to be produced and exceptional mills to become listed buildings based on their architectural or townscape merits, work which English Heritage and subsequently Historic England ultimately took forward.

Although the SAVE report strongly advocated the preservation of mills, it was somewhat vague as to what their future role should be – there was an assumption that other industrial or workspace uses would be found for retained mills. An exemplar case study was, however, included in the report, giving details of how an area of Lowell, Massachusetts, a former mill town, had been designated a National Historic Park and visitor attraction. Clearly though, at the time the report was published, the idea that mills could be converted to residential uses and people would actually want to live in what were then run-down inner-city areas was beyond any stretch of the imagination.

Following the wholescale closure of textile manufacturing businesses, mills became vacant or were used for small workshops, warehousing, furniture factories, cash-and-carry outlets and mail-order business etc. These were characterised by town planners, somewhat disapprovingly, as 'twilight uses', and it was largely assumed they were temporary and transitionary by nature. Many mills were only partially occupied, with upper floors often abandoned due to limited lift access and concerns as to whether the cast iron columns could support modern heavy plant equipment.

The advent of inner-city policies and funding schemes in the late 1970s and early 1980s, such as the Department of Environment's Urban Programme, enabled local authorities to access central government funding to refurbish industrial buildings, including mills, to create workshop units up to 2,500 sq ft, business space not provided by the commercial property sector.

Subsequent urban regeneration policies during the 1980s onwards brought forward a plethora of government and European structural funding regimes administered by a succession of organisations such as local authorities, English Partnerships, regional development agencies and Local Enterprise Partnerships. However, these were targeted at a wider property-led regeneration agenda, with none specifically aimed at addressing the issue of vacant mills. However, such funding sources were utilised to fund the abnormal cost elements of mill renovation projects such as the Old and New Sedgwick mills and Royal Mills redevelopment in Ancoats, Manchester. ING Real Estate undertook these mill residential conversions between 2004 and 2006, using both European Regional Development and North West Regional Development Agency funding contributions.

Voluntary groups also played a significant role in preserving abandoned mills in their local neighbourhoods. Ancoats Building Preservation Trust in Manchester successfully campaigned for the retention of important historic mills such as Murrays' Mills, while other entrepreneurial not-for-profit organisations also became the catalysts for wider-scale mill renovation schemes. Leigh Building Preservation Trust initially secured a small grant and recruited volunteers to restore the steam engine and repair the engine house at Leigh Spinners Mill, before embarking on further projects aimed at securing the future of the mill.

Historic England has since taken the lead in highlighting the issue of vacant mills and the potential benefits of renovating such buildings to bring them back into productive use. In 2016 Historic England produced separate reports for Yorkshire and the North West entitled *Engines of Prosperity: New Uses for Old Mills*. The reports assessed the scale of vacant properties, calculated the potential job and housing units which they could accommodate if repurposed, highlighted good-practice lessons, and made a broad series of recommendations aimed at partner organisations.

The championing role adopted by Historic England and the national publicity generated by the reports appear to have stimulated significant interest and discussions with a number of public-sector funding organisations, mill owners and developers.

In 2018, West Yorkshire Combined Authority commissioned a *Feasibility and Investment Framework* for ten priority mill sites in West Yorkshire. The final report identified intervention options and the anticipated level of investment for each of the respective mill developments. The report provided the justification and rationale for WYCA's subsequent financial support to several schemes, including

- Conditioning House, Bradford – A £1.5 million contribution towards enabling works for the conversion of Conditioning House, a Grade II listed Victorian warehouse which had been empty for 25 years. The scheme created 133 flats and commercial floorspace.

- Rutland Mills, Wakefield – A £2.89 million contribution towards the restoration and conversion of five mill buildings as part of the first phase of converting 'Wakefield Waterfront into a diverse and multi-functional cultural landmark for the north'.

The report also led to the creation of a West Yorkshire Mills Redevelopment Working Group to coordinate the work of five West Yorkshire local authorities, WYCA, Homes England, and Historic England.

In 2021 Historic England published *Driving Northern Growth Through Repurposing Historic Mills*,[37] which revised and updated the previous *Engines of Prosperity: New Uses for Old Mills reports*[38] for both Yorkshire and the North West. Although considerable progress had been made in regenerating mills, the reports concluded that

- 688 mills were still vacant or underutilised, offering substantive scope for redevelopment (293 in Greater Manchester, 237 in Yorkshire, and 158 in Pennine Lancashire);

- Cumulatively, these mills offered approximately 2.25 million sq m of vacant floor space (1.1 million sq m in Greater Manchester, 750,000 sq m in Yorkshire, and 400,000 sq m in Pennine Lancashire).

If all of the vacant mills across the north were developed for residential use, Historic England estimated they could accommodate approximately

- 42,400 homes; 13,000 apartments in Greater Manchester, almost 9,000 in Yorkshire and nearly 5,000 in Pennine Lancashire, and a further 15,400 homes on surplus land.

- 83,600 jobs; 41,500 in Greater Manchester, 27,600 in Yorkshire, and 14,500 in Pennine Lancashire. (On the basis that mills were redeveloped with an equal mix of office and light industrial uses.)

- Add £3 billion of gross value to the local economy.

Fig 4.2 Mill sunrise, Bents Mill.

Oldham Council case study

Oldham is a fascinating example of how attitudes and approaches towards vacant mills have changed over time within a local authority – from policies of demolition in the 1970s to proactive restoration in the 2020s. Oldham became the leading cotton mill town during the two great cotton booms of 1873–5 and 1904–8. Oldham, 'the cotton spinning capital of the world', had at one time over 200 mills within its boundaries.[39] In 1977 Oldham Council decided to adopt a mill clearance policy as part of a comprehensive redevelopment plan to create vacant land for new investment:

> The Oldham Economic Development and Publicity Subcommittee has … considered the ways in which Oldham is handicapped by there still being about 140 mills in the town. Many mills are unsightly and deny the use of the site to more modern premises … the subcommittee has … considered that efforts should be made to largely clear Oldham of mills by the end of the century. Clearance of 100 mills in the Borough would clearly largely deal with the problem at an estimated net cost of £2.6 million.[40]

Oldham's original plan was to demolish about 150 mills, releasing 700 acres of land for new development and to permit only the most modern and fully occupied mills to remain. This would be achieved by a private act of Parliament which would define a set of standards (for example, sufficient parking), which if not met would mean mills could be condemned as 'unfit' and obsolete for modern uses.[41] Oldham Council would be given powers to acquire and demolish such mills and sell the sites for new industry regardless of whether they were in use or not. Such a policy was, in effect, an industrial version of the large-scale slum housing clearance schemes previously undertaken in many inner-city areas across the north.

This approach appears to have been largely driven by the negative image it was felt the mills projected of the town and the belief that they should make way for new industrial developments more befitting a technological era. The policy is also a reflection of planning policies of the time and a preoccupation with single-use zoning and a desire to separate industrial and residential areas which were seen as being uncomplementary. The prevailing viewpoint was that given the decline of manufacturing industries, the coming high-tech and service-based sectors of the future would occupy new purpose-built business parks on the periphery of towns. Such business estates would have extensive parking, be accessed by new orbital roads and be located far from residential areas. In short, the antithesis of the commercial space 'offer' provided by mills.

As well as completely disregarding the heritage, historic and townscape values of Oldham mills, the clearance policies also ignored the fact that many provided a valuable source of cheap flexible accommodation for small businesses offering low-skill employment, as well as providing 'incubator' space for business start-ups.

Oldham soon discovered that given the sheer number of mills and the costs involved, it was unable to raise sufficient funding to acquire and demolish the mills and the legislation was not pursued.

Over 40 years later, Oldham's approach has gone full circle, with the council becoming one of the few local authorities to develop a dedicated strategy aimed at retaining and regenerating its mills: 'the mill stock forms a fundamental part of Oldham's historic environment and gives the landscape of the Borough a clear distinctive character thereby contributing to local identity and sense of place'.[42]

At the time the Mills Strategy was commissioned, 106 mills remained in Oldham. The process behind the plan was to first assess the mills in the context of their contribution to council regeneration priorities, landscape impact, heritage importance, and housing and employment potential. Based on such assessments, a prioritisation was then made of each mill, awarding them a high, medium and low prioritisation. Areas with a critical mass or clusters of mills formed part of the selection criteria in cases where they 'provide a unique character to the local landscape and give Oldham an exceptionally strong sense of place and local distinctiveness'.

The strategy report identifies 22 mills as being of high priority and 26 of medium priority. Given the current local government funding regime and loss of central government support, local authorities such as Oldham Council clearly do not have significant capital funding to invest in mill development projects. In this context the report makes a series of recommendations as to how the council can use its role as the local planning authority to safeguard mills rather than acting as a funder or developer. Such ideas include using the planning system and enforcement powers to make it more difficult for developers to demolish priority mills, the designation of identified mill clusters as conservation areas, environmental improvements such as mill streetscape projects, and a marketing strategy to promote both the existing mill stock as having affordable employment and residential potential especially in the context of Oldham's transport connections within Greater Manchester.

Oldham provides one potential local authority approach to mill preservation and redevelopment. We will examine other models in Chapter 5.

Design codes

In addition to commissioning mill strategies, another form of intervention is the production of a mill design code aimed at providing developers with guidance as to the types of schemes a local authority would like to see brought forward.

Historic England and Pendle Borough Council have commissioned the production of a Pendle Textile Mills Design Code. Design codes aim to achieve high-quality design and good conservation practice by producing a set of illustrated design requirements providing parameters for the physical development of a site or area.

This project will cover the 93 textile mills in the area and will focus on a number of in-depth case studies including mills in Brierfield, Colne, Nelson and Barnoldswick.

The role of cultural regeneration

A number of the early mill regeneration schemes in the 1980s, such as Dean Clough and Salts Mill, differentiated their offers by using arts and culture as the foundations for their regeneration proposals.

Subsequent theories on emerging 'knowledge industries' and Richard Florida's creative class research[43] argued for the nurturing of 'cultural industries' to be at the heart of future local economies and job creation. Influenced by the success of Dean Clough and Salts Mill and such prevailing local economic development theories, many local authority and voluntary-sector organisations latched on to these concepts and based their public-sector funding bids around the idea of regenerating mills to accommodate and foster 'creative clusters'.

Similarly, developers faced with launching schemes in peripheral 'edgy' areas of towns and cities with weak property markets often initially encouraged artists to occupy spaces within their buildings to create activity within what would otherwise be large areas of vacant

MILL FIRES

Throughout the Industrial Revolution mill fires were a frequent occurrence due to the combination of timber-framed buildings, flammable materials and the widespread use of candles, which were the only source of light.

However, even in modern times mills still seem to burn down with alarming frequency – as one newspaper headline put it, 'Another day, another devastating fire at a derelict mill in Yorkshire'.[69]

Historic England found that there had been over 100 fires at derelict mills in Bradford alone since 2010. One of the most high-profile recent fires is that of Dalton Mills in Keighley, which was gutted in 2022 with virtually only the building façade remaining of the mill fronting onto Dalton Lane. Other mills suffering various degrees of fire damage over the last decade have included Ebor Mill in Haworth, Drummonds Mill in Bradford, Prospect Mills in Thornton (three fires in a five-year period), Newsome Mill in Huddersfield, Bank Bottom Mill in Marsden, and so the list goes on.

Why do mills suffer disproportionately from incidents of fires? In the first instance, mills are full of flammable materials which have accumulated such as dust, grease and oil from machinery, discarded fibres, and lanolin from sheep's wool, all of which have soaked into timber beams and wooden floors. Many mills are semi-derelict and poorly secured, meaning they can be accessed by vandals and rough sleepers who light fires for warmth. Arson is a major contributory factor, with a number of recent prosecutions for serial offenders.

The use of mills for illegal purposes is also a source of fire damage. During 2021 West Yorkshire Police dismantled over 1,000 cannabis farms, a number of which were in mill buildings.[70] Such operations involve the use of highly dangerous DIY electrical wiring systems which are major fire risks.

Mill fires are so frequent that they can be the basis for local conspiracy theories, especially given some listed mills occupy potentially lucrative brownfield development sites which will only be realised if a mill's condition deteriorates to a point where demolition becomes inevitable. Indeed, one mill-owning interviewee dryly speculated as to whether a local developer who had had three fires at their mills employed an 'in-house arsonist as part of their development team'.

Left Dalton Mills, Keighley.

Below Police uncover cannabis farm in West Yorkshire mill.

floorspace. The presence of groups of artists has been part of a wider city gentrification process repositioning neighbourhoods as 'cool' rather than threatening, altering perceptions and gaining wider buy-in needed to attract more affluent residents and tenants.

As property demand increases, unless there is substantial available space, creative workers can ultimately find themselves forced out by other competing higher-value uses. Artists such as those at Linden Mills, Hebden Bridge, can find themselves under notice of eviction when the owner develops plans to convert the mill to apartments. Ironically, artists can be the victims of rising property prices which their presence has helped to create.

However, terminologies have evolved, and the term 'cultural industries' has been superseded by 'creative industries' and more recently 'the commercial creative sector'. A number of the early public-sector-funded mill renovation projects, aimed at attracting 'cultural industry' businesses, appear to have aspired to become the home of high-profile, high-growth, cutting-edge video, film, TV and computer-gaming production company tenants. Instead, many have attracted low-growth arts-based businesses such as part-time, self-employed painters, photographers, jewellers and potters. There is clearly a difficult trade-off between holding one's nerve and sticking with the original vision for a centre aimed at supporting creative industry businesses and therefore turning away prospective tenant businesses who fall outside this target sector, versus the need to fill vacant commercial space and generate income by accepting any business able to pay the rent.

Sunny Bank Mills

Sunny Bank Mills, Farsley near Leeds, has been in the Gaunt family for 150 years. Following the end of textile production, cousins John and William Gaunt decided early on that cultural regeneration would play a key role in the future of the mill complex. According to John, 'The cultural side was always our intention – we were a creative place when we were manufacturing textiles.'[44] The two cornerstones of the mill's cultural regeneration are the art gallery, which has a programme of exhibitions and events supporting regional artists, and a historical archive charting the mill's history and the stories of the people who worked there. The archive has become one of the most important and substantial of its type in the UK.

Fig 4.3 Artist's studio, Sunny Bank Mills.

Since 2012 the mill has hosted 75 exhibitions, supporting over 1,000 artists and makers and now receives over 500,000 annual visitors. The mill was designed to maximise natural light so consequently has numerous well-lit spaces perfect for artists to create and display their works (**Fig 4.3**). The Old Woollen Building,

Fig 4.4 Tileyard North, Wakefield.

built in 1830, has now been turned into a 500-seat music and comedy live performance space by events company Trouble at Mill.

In summary, according to John Gaunt, 'creative placemaking uses the power of art and culture to reinvigorate our mill communities and its spaces'.[45]

Tileyard, Wakefield

Tileyard North is a further example of a creative-sector-led regeneration project based on the transformation of Rutland Mills and the area adjacent to the Hepworth Museum in Wakefield.

Rutland Mills is a Grade II listed mill complex which was a hub for worsted spinning and knitting yarn, but has been vacant since 1999. Work is now underway to create Tileyard North, a 135,000 sq ft creative industries hub, the UK's largest outside London.

Developer Paul Kempe's vision for Rutland Mills is 'a vibrant regional destination for creative and collaborative partnerships in music, film, TV, design, new media and indeed all facets of the commercial creative sector'.[46] The aim behind the scheme is to replicate the successful Tileyard London community of independent artists and businesses established in an area around Kings Cross: 'Tileyard is the world's largest creative community'.

Tileyard North will be 'home to 500+ new creative jobs' and will involve the creation of a music hub, hotel, education and arts facilities, and an indoor market incorporating bars, restaurants and cafés modelled on the Time Out Market in Lisbon. The redevelopment involves the demolition of two buildings – the first to create a new public square and the second to open up access to the River Calder, a key element of Wakefield's 10-acre waterfront regeneration master plan (**Figs 4.4, 5.10**).

CASE STUDY

Gibson Mill

Gibson Mill was built in 1803 by Abraham Gibson, and is situated within Hardcastle Crags woodland near to Hebden Bridge.

In 1902 Gibson Mill was transformed into an 'entertainment emporium' offering a dance hall, dining room and boating on the mill pond. After the Second World War, a roller skating rink was installed in the weaving shed with lessons provided by Arnold Binns, a world-champion skater. The mill slipped into decline until in 1950 Lord Savile gifted the mill and 214 acres of land to the National Trust.

Gibson Mill has since been converted into a self-sufficient off-grid environmental education visitor centre and sustainability showcase. Electricity is provided via a hydro system utilising the mill's 1926 turbine. A smaller turbine is also used during periods when water levels are low. Solar thermal panels and solar photovoltaic panels, installed along the ridgeline of the mill, combine to provide hot water and electricity, while a system of batteries stores surplus generated electricity. A log-burning stove and boiler provide cooking, hot water and space heating. The mill also uses the natural spring water from Hardcastle Crags as its water supply.

According to the National Trust, 'the mill is 100% self-sufficient in energy, water and waste treatment. The combination of technologies used, the size of the building and the fact that it does not link up to the National Grid, make the mill unique in Great Britain.'[56]

Mill pond reflections.

Visitor Centre.

Gibson Mill.

Higherford Mill

Higherford Mill at Barrowford is a listed spinning mill built in 1824. In 1832 steam power was introduced to supplement the water power and a chimney was built, with a flue running up the adjoining hillside. The mill continued to use water power in conjunction with steam power until the late 19th century. The main weaving shed has since become one of the oldest surviving in the world.

The mill ceased production in 1971 and was then sold. The new owner converted part of the mill to workspace units, with the rest of the building becoming derelict. In December 1994 an application was submitted for consent to demolish the mill and build housing. Villagers and Heritage Trust for the North West objected, and after a five-year campaign the Trust purchased the mill in 1999.

Higherford Mill has since become a focal point for the creative industries of East Lancashire. Workshops have been constructed in the old weaving sheds which currently provide space to 20 businesses. Plans are being developed to create a Cultural Heritage Centre with interpretation materials and visitor facilities.

Above Centre for Creative Industries.

Left Machinery exhibits.

Opposite Higherford Mill.

HIGHERFORD MILL

Lomeshaye Bridge Mill

Lomeshaye Bridge Mill in Nelson was originally a two-storey steam-powered cotton spinning mill dating back to 1841. Two further storeys and the adjoining weaving sheds were added in 1899.

The mill is located adjacent to the Leeds and Liverpool Canal and predates the construction of the adjoining Whitefield model village, now a conservation area, with St Mary's Church as its focal point.

Lomeshaye Bridge Mill was purchased by the Heritage Trust for the North West in 1998 following a local campaign to remove both the mill and Victorian terraced housing from a comprehensive redevelopment scheme. The Prince of Wales' Regeneration Trust adopted the mill as an exemplar project and supported efforts to work with the local community to find sustainable new uses for the building. A Heritage Lottery Fund Townscape Heritage Initiative grant supported the £1 million conversion project.

Work started in 2014 to convert the mill to workspace, archive storage and a workshop for the Trust's Conservation Services. Tenant rents provide an income for the Heritage Trust for the North West, and help support its wider portfolio of projects.

Above and opposite
Lomeshaye Bridge Mill.

Dale End Mill

Dale End Mill is a Grade II* listed mill located close to the Pennine Way at Lothersdale. In 1792 Thomas Parker converted the mill from corn grinding to textile manufacturing and by 1835 the mill was given over to worsted spinning. The subsequent expansion of the mill, including the addition of weaving sheds in the 1850s, created the need for a larger waterwheel supplemented by a steam engine and the addition of a 90ft chimney.

In 1852 James Ellison designed and built the magnificent 45-foot-diameter suspension wheel. The wheel at Dale End Mill is reputed to be the largest indoor waterwheel in the world and a superb example of the millwright's craft. The waterwheel and steam engine together provided the power for 190 looms and 1,700 spindles. The waterwheel was powered via a mill pond within the village channelled through a goit (a narrow channel) and linking to the beck which runs directly under the mill.

The remains of a Green's Economiser can also be seen, stacks of metal pipes arranged in the flues leading from the boiler to the chimney. Designed by Edward Green, the Economiser made savings by utilising the exhaust gases from the boiler furnace to heat boiler feed water, pumped through the pipes, thereby reducing the energy needed to produce steam.

The mill covers 36,000 sq ft, including weaving sheds of 18,000 sq ft. Four generations of the Wilson family owned and managed the mill prior to its purchase in 1981 by June Barrow as part of a partnership. June was determined to conserve the building for the benefit of the village. Parts of the mill were subsequently used for furniture retail, storage and other warehouse uses.

June's son Jon Barrow is now single-handedly restoring the mill to create three holiday units, a variety of commercial workshops for artisan businesses and other potential uses.

Window view.

Above Jon Barrow.

Right Fire extinguisher.

Above Work to be done.

Left Dale End Mill.

Horace Mills

Guy Taylor, architect and managing director of Candelisa, had previously been involved in refurbishing three mills before starting work on regenerating Horace Mills, a landmark building in Cononley, near Skipton. The scheme has created high-quality apartments and housing at the mill site adjoining Cononley train station.

The mill had been derelict for a number of years and the scheme involved building a new parallel block with a cantilever structure to support the original mill, together with the creation of a new annexe. The mill restoration was cross-subsidised by new housing built on the former warehouse site behind the mill.

Guy's interest in development stems from visiting sites as a youngster with his civil engineer father. Being both an architect and developer has given him the opportunity for greater control across the whole design and build process and the chance to undertake innovative and higher-risk mill schemes which other developers would not consider.

Above Guy Taylor.

Opposite Mill at night.

Douglas Mill

Douglas Mill is a Grade II listed mill and coach house, built in the 1840s on Bowling Old Lane, Bradford.

The mill has been refurbished by Kier to create teaching facilities for the Dixons Sixth Form Academy. A key consideration in the building's selection was its location and accessibility for inner-city communities in the heart of Bradford. Work began on the £13.3 million project in December 2018 and was completed in spring 2020. Restoration challenges included repurposing the listed coach house, which had been unoccupied for 20 years, to create changing facilities for an adjoining new-build sports hall, and designing a dining area within a basement space.

The refurbishment retains the mill's original features such as corridors of columns and original brickwork. Nearly all rooms benefit from natural light from the mill fenestration patterns on the front and exterior elevations. The building has a modern, light, airy feel and provides high-quality accommodation for the 850 students studying at the Academy.

Right Douglas Mill.

Below Old and new.

DIXONS
SIXTH FORM
ACADEMY

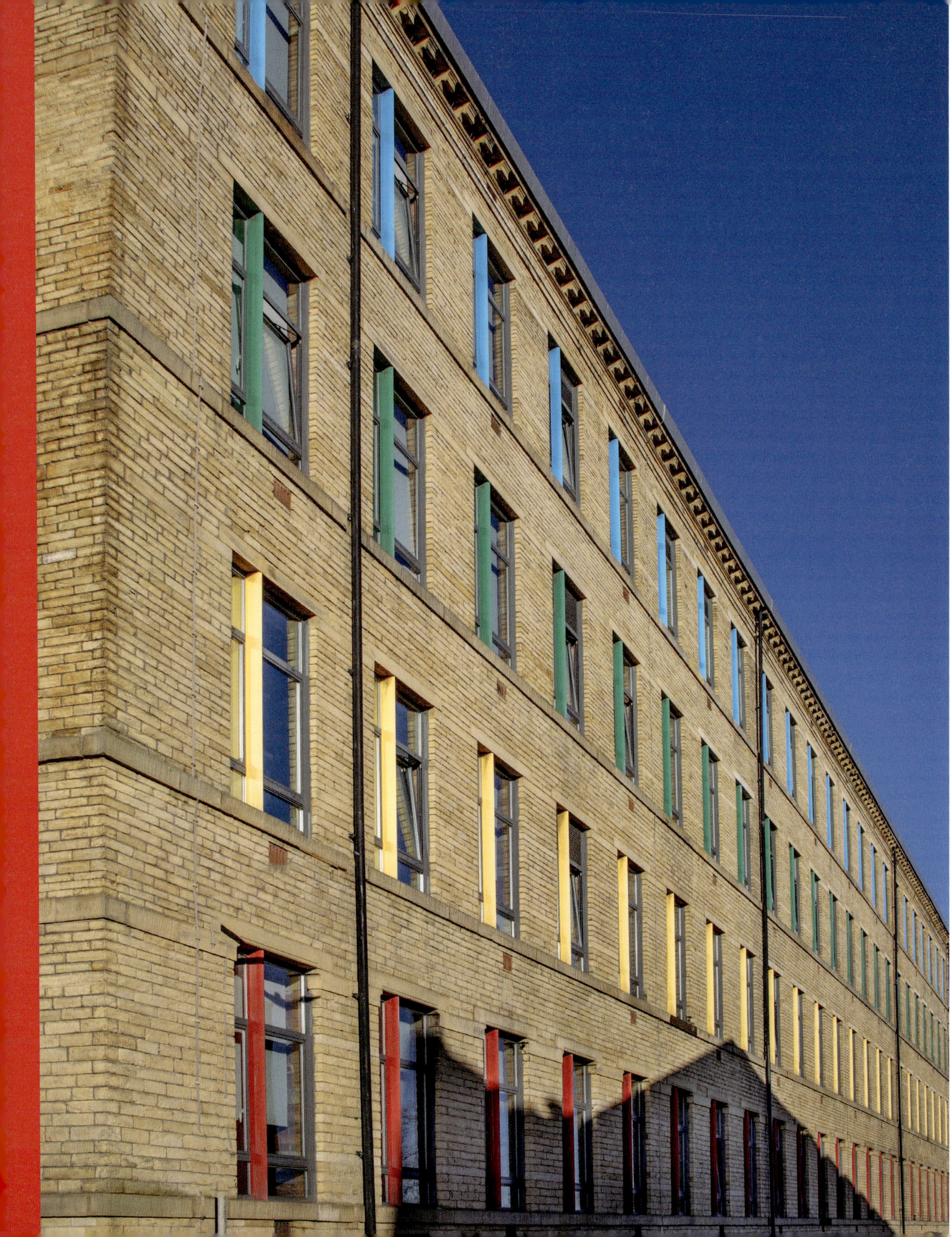

Façade.

Columns.

5

The mill development process

In this chapter we will examine the process by which mills are renovated and repurposed. First, we will make an examination of the differing types of mill developers and their characteristics. This will draw on interviews held with many of the key players involved in the 31 mill development projects visited as part of the book research. We will then consider the role of the various professional actors and organisations involved in the development process, together with their respective insights and perspectives. Finally, we will draw conclusions as to the types of practical measures needed to catalyse further mill regeneration schemes.

Mill renovators – Leadership traits

During the case study visits, it became apparent that behind each successful mill restoration there were invariably one or two key individuals who had the initial vision and then provided the leadership and drive to deliver these complex schemes. Such mill renovators are drawn from a wide range of backgrounds, but share a number of character traits. They

- are attracted to the challenge of preserving a unique building, and this evolves into an emotional commitment and a sense of civic duty to bring about the preservation of a local landmark. For many, the restoration of a mill is a life-time's work, spanning years and becomes their personal legacy. They develop a bond with the mill and invest something of themselves in restoring these buildings.

- have enormous tenacity and persistence in overcoming the financial and administrative hurdles, cynicism and negativity often associated with undertaking large-scale building restoration projects.

- see a range of opportunities in such spaces but manage to keep to an overall master plan rather than becoming distracted chasing multiple competing ideas.

- have an overall vision and plan for the building but are able to segment work into bite-size viable chunks and not spread their efforts too thinly. They remain focused on achievable, incremental, small-scale projects within the overall development master plan.

- invest an enormous amount of personal and financial capital in the restoration and repurposing of their mill. Such commitments often extend well beyond a logical business planning approach. Above all, they have an appetite for risk.

- regard themselves more as custodians rather than owners of their respective mills. They are conscious of their role as being one of many who have shaped the mill's history over multiple generations.

- honour and celebrate the building's history by preserving as many architectural and historical elements as possible within the mill renovation scheme.

- are adept at 'getting people onside' and building relationships with regulatory bodies to secure necessary permissions and consents. Their enthusiasm and commitment to the project is often persuasive and infectious.

- envisage future uses for their mill but are not bound by rigid constraints. They adopt a flexible approach to future uses or tenants for the mill during the renovation phases, while gaining insights into the local property market to hone and position a distinct offer within it.

- learn new skills such as project management, financial, budgetary and construction work to achieve their renovation goals.

- prioritise spending on necessities rather than 'nice to haves' which have limited impact and consume scarce resources.

- create early income streams, for example workspaces or holiday lets, which help with cash flow and generate further investment in their renovation scheme.

- are *funding fed* rather than *funding led*. They secure grants and other public funding when appropriate but do not allow themselves to become dependent on, or distracted by, chasing public support to take forward their scheme.

- take advice and build relations with key agencies but do not allow officials, consultants or advisors, with 'no skin in the game', to dictate the agenda.

- work hard at keeping the local community involved and informed to build local ownership and commitment to the project.

- are often somewhat possessive and protective of their mill project and have concerns as to what will happen in future years to their legacy. For some individual owners there is a worry as to whether others will be prepared to take on the time and financial commitments involved in maintaining and running their mill. An overriding concern is whether, at a future date, the building will be acquired by 'faceless developers' intent on redeveloping the mill site in an unsympathetic manner to maximise profits.

- learn from others. They spend time networking and learning lessons from other mill renovation projects.

It is clear from these shared characteristics and values that leadership skills, entrepreneurialism, risk-taking and tenacity are prerequisites for successful mill restoration projects.

It has also become apparent that such individuals tend to operate within three distinct and different organisational structures:

1 Commercial property developers who acquire mills to undertake bespoke residential or commercial development schemes. Given their profit-making nature, such schemes inevitably take place in areas with strong housing or commercial property markets.

2 Individuals or close-knit family groups who have embarked on long-term restorations of mills in their ownership. In most cases the owners have an emotional bond to the mill based on family history or local connections. Such projects vary in scale, ranging from small mills in rural village settings to large urban mill complexes.

3 Voluntary-sector or not-for-profit organisations who have campaigned to renovate a specific mill, recruited volunteers, secured grants, and often taken on the management of a mill to provide community facilities and employment space. Such groups include Leigh Building Preservation Trust (Leigh Spinners Mill), Heritage Trust for the North West (Lomeshaye Bridge and Higherford mills) and Castleton Heritage Trust (Queens Mill).

Insights

The process of mill regeneration is ongoing; because of their size, flexibility and central locations, mills will continue to be repurposed to meet emerging needs and societal demands. Mills have been around for over 200 years and will, in future years, accommodate activities which currently cannot be predicted or envisaged. Considerable progress has been made in recent years in recognising the historic and potential asset value of mills and bringing about successful renovation schemes. However, given there are still over 680 vacant or underutilised mills in Yorkshire and Lancashire alone, considerable work is still required to save and repurpose mills throughout the UK.

In the first instance it is worth considering the views from the three categories of mill renovators as to the measures they believe will encourage further mill transformations. We will then consider the role of public support agencies and what further actions can be undertaken to support future mill renovations.

1. Commercial property developers' perspective

Although every mill is unique, the case studies and interviews reveal a number of shared similarities in relation to the approach of commercial property developers and the lessons they have learnt. These can be summarised as follows:

- Mills have charisma and character. Successful developers have targeted mills located in areas with strong property markets. Most commercial schemes have identified vacant mills in established housing market areas such as those within or in close proximity to Manchester and Leeds. Such schemes can achieve a return without the need for any public-sector gap funding. However, mill conversions in secondary towns have the same build costs but greatly reduced sale and rental values compared to the major cities. This makes it extremely difficult to achieve viability and secure investors in peripheral locations.

- In such cases, mill development schemes will be dependent on securing gap funding or some imaginative financial investment arrangement with a local authority. Despite widespread austerity, different pots of public money are still available and can be harnessed to achieve viability. In many cases such funding sources remain unspent because of the lack of good-quality worked-up schemes. An astute developer will spend time identifying potential sources of gap funding and cultivate relationships with grant-awarding bodies. However, grant funding comes with strings attached and takes significant time and effort to secure.

- Finding building contractors who are prepared to undertake mill schemes is becoming increasingly difficult. Many contractors much prefer to work on new-build schemes where there are far fewer risks. Issues such as the mill's structural integrity, presence of asbestos etc, only become apparent once works have begun.

- However well planned, the lengthy timescale for mill conversions, from acquisition to completion, coupled with recent above-inflation increases in building materials, means that it is extremely difficult to keep schemes within budget and to accurately predict the final return on any development scheme.

- It is becoming more difficult to retain old historic features within mills. For example, in the case of the Old Town Mill near Hebden Bridge, a number of the old original timber beams had to be boxed in to prevent heat loss and noise transfer between apartments. Retaining original features of historic buildings is becoming more difficult in the light of changes in building regulations since the Grenfell fire disaster. In the case of Crusader Mill in Manchester, developers Capital & Centric have been forced to cover the original oak floors in order to mitigate fire risks.

- Early engagement with the local authority is vital to secure support for a project. It is essential to build relationships with planners, conservation officers and Historic England, whose support is crucial if the scheme is to progress.

- There is a perception among developers that planning gain tariffs are imposed in an arbitrary and inconsistent manner across local authorities, with widely varying approaches towards Section 106 and Community Infrastructure Levy payment planning conditions (*see* 'Planning system' on p. 136).

- Undertaking selective demolition of buildings on the mill site can lead to the creation of a viable scheme. New-build housing within the site curtilage may often cross-subsidise the renovation of the main mill buildings. In many cases this has led to planning consent negotiations regarding the demolition of a mill's single-storey weaving sheds which occupy a large footprint, are difficult to convert to other uses and have limited commercial and architectural value. Even when new build is not feasible, weaving sheds or ancillary buildings have often been demolished to facilitate car parking and improve access and circulation space or public realm features. There are, however, a few examples of weaving and combing sheds with their distinctive north-light roofs being converted to housing (**Fig 5.1**).

- Scheme phasing. When occupied mills are being transitioned to new uses, a carefully managed phased approach is needed to relocate tenants into specific spaces on the site while works are undertaken. This maintains occupancy levels and creates an income stream to fund conversion works on vacant buildings from which tenants have been decanted. In the case of Sunny Bank Mills, this self-financing model has been the only option given financial institutions are reluctant to invest in mills dedicated to employment rather than residential uses.

Fig 5.1 Weaving shed residential conversion, Stansfield Mill Lane, Triangle.

- Expect the unexpected. When undertaking large-scale renovations on historic buildings, the challenges will often only become apparent when work begins and issues are uncovered. Therefore, contingency budgets and flexible timescales need to be incorporated into scheme business planning.

- The cost of the necessary surveys and technical reports can be substantial and needs to be budgeted for in advance. To support a listed mill planning application, it may be necessary to commission a heritage statement and reports examining conservation, biodiversity, environmental impacts, drainage, structural issues and so on.

- Residents have increased expectations about the green features they expect in their new homes such as solar panels, electric vehicle charge points, low-carbon heating, and insulation levels exceeding minimum standards. These add costs to schemes but bring no additional returns to the developer. Residents paying a premium for a mill apartment also have expectations regarding individual garden or patio areas which are difficult to provide in many schemes.

- Retail spaces. Large, deep floorplates can be successfully utilised to create successful retail floorspaces. Good examples of this are Red Brick Mill in Batley and Pendle Village Mill with department store-style layouts.

- Managed mills apartment schemes. There are a small number of niche development companies who are undertaking build-to-let schemes, creating mill

Fig 5.2 Mill letting board, Skipton.

apartments in desirable property market areas to satisfy a growing demand for high-end rented accommodation while building a property portfolio for foreign investors, for example Greenholme Mills in Burley in Wharfedale.

- Apartments must be of a decent size and quality and the building well maintained. One mill developer was critical of other schemes for creating 'tiny flats with no lobbies and a high turnover of tenants'. If a mill is not developed sympathetically with imaginative design and quality materials, it can date quite quickly and require expensive ongoing maintenance.

- Mill regeneration projects should not be predicated on securing public-sector funding. Grant or loan funding often comes with strings attached and takes significant time and effort to secure. It is a 'nice to have', but chasing public funding can become a distraction and leaves the destiny of the scheme in the hands of local officials or civil servants.

- Build a brand and connect with the local community. It is essential to have a strong communications strategy, not only to build a scheme brand and attract future occupants but to also engage and keep local people onside. This can involve public site visits, open days, social media presence, capturing human-interest stories from people whose relatives once worked in the mill or, for example, the establishment of the Sunny Bank Mill Archive, which is run by volunteers.

- Sales and lettings are relatively easy – there is a strong demand for heritage buildings and only a limited supply (**Fig 5.2**).

Fig 5.3 Dale End Mill.

From discussions with the respective commercial developers, it is apparent that they take great pride in restoring such historic buildings and creating an asset for future generations. The architectural heritage aspects of such buildings differentiate cities and towns and create a sense of place and history. The positive feedback received from local people on the mill renovation, its former history and their mill-related anecdotes is a source of satisfaction. In an industry where the quality of design and construction of new-build housing is often criticised, it is a source of great satisfaction to work on mill conversions; for many it will be a highlight of their careers.

Developers will continue to be attracted to mills coming onto the market in 'decent areas' which show a good return. There is also evidence of one developer securing foreign investment to create high-end mill apartments for rent rather than for sale. In such cases mill developments will take place without any public-sector support.

The issue is how to get developers to consider investing in mills where the local property market is weak. Few developers have an appetite for, or are able to secure investors in, high-risk market-making 'build-it-and-they-will-come' projects.

In terms of suggestions as to what can be done to bring forward further mill conversions, the commercial developers interviewed were mainly concerned that planning issues were dealt with speedily and there is greater flexibility in relation to affordable housing contributions (*see* 'Planning system' on p. 136). In terms of instigating mill conversions in weak property market areas, it was felt that the public sector has a role in de-risking such projects and providing a range of support schemes to enable one or two schemes to get underway which might establish a market and give sufficient confidence to encourage others to make follow-on investments.

2. Mills in family or individual ownership

As previously identified, there is a small niche group of mill renovators who have inherited or acquired mills and are painstakingly restoring them. Whereas 20 years ago it may have been possible to buy a vacant and semi-derelict mill at a nominal amount to embark on a 'Grand Designs' project, such opportunities are now much more limited. In areas where house prices remain high, commercial developers are now much more willing to consider mill conversions and this is reflected in increased market valuations which largely preclude individual buyers from acquiring mills.

However, there are still a surprising number of individuals and family groups who retain ownership of mills and are committed to restoring them over many years. In the case of Jon Barrow, who is single-handedly restoring Dale End Mill at Lothersdale, this will be a life-time's endeavour (**Fig 5.3**). Such entrepreneurs are primarily self-sufficient and will quietly get on with the mill renovation in hand, ideally without the interference of others.

The general impression gained was that such individuals were sceptical about chasing 'here-today-gone-tomorrow' grant funding that would inevitably be time consuming to secure and would come with strings attached. However, it does appear that for some it is a lonely life and the chance to meet other like-minded individuals would be welcome. Indeed, requests were made on a number of occasions for information and contacts for other mills developer counterparts who had been visited as part of the book's research.

William and John Gaunt took time to visit successful mill conversions before beginning work on the regeneration of Sunny Bank Mills and try to visit different mills each year. They participated in events such as a national mills regeneration conference and have developed links with local history groups.

There would appear to be value in a series of networking events and visits targeted at individual mill renovators, together with the possibility of an annual mill regeneration conference.

3. Not-for-profit organisations

Voluntary and community-sector organisations, including housing associations, have often played an important campaigning and lobbying role preventing the demolition of mills at a time when statutory bodies have been uninterested. These groups have become a direct communication link to the wider local community, have obtained grants and recruited substantial numbers of volunteers to undertake painstaking renovation works. In the case of the Leigh Building Preservation Trust, their restoration of the original steam engine and engine house at Leigh Spinners Mill led to their involvement in further large-scale renovation projects at the mill (**Fig 5.4**).

Providing sustained leadership over a protracted period is difficult, especially given that many of the organisations' committee trustee roles are time consuming and unpaid.

Mill conversions undertaken by community organisations can often date back 20–30 years, to a time when public-sector grant funding was more readily available. The scheme originators are usually no longer employed by the organisation and the mill management is now undertaken by staff who were not part of the original project design process. A number of such projects visited

Fig 5.4 Leigh Spinners Mill.

Fig 5.5 Construction works, Old Town.

during the research often appeared to have large amounts of vacant or under-utilised space. In such cases the original mill concept needs to be revisited and their offer refreshed in the light of changing markets and trends. The process of mill regeneration is ongoing. New people responsible for managing and developing mill buildings need to be given the headroom to bring forward fresh ideas as to how previously repurposed mills can be again transitioned to meet changing requirements.

Easy access to small-scale grants to undertake early-stage project feasibility studies and fund communication materials, and social media marketing support to achieve wider-scale community engagement were all highlighted as being of particular value.

Construction procurement process

An issue of increasing concern to all mill developers is that of accurately forecasting major construction costs. To place this in context, it is worth considering the process by which a mill owner/developer procures construction works (**Fig 5.5**).

In simplistic terms, the process for a mill regeneration project is as follows:

1. Clearly, if the mill is not in the ownership of the developer, they will need to reach an agreement for the future purchase of the mill before spending time on working up a scheme proposal. There are numerous permutations as to how this can be achieved, ranging from a straightforward purchase contract, an option agreement with sale completion and price dependent on securing planning consent, staged payment arrangements, or in some cases even a right of 'first refusal' if a developer cannot persuade a landowner to enter into a binding commitment.

2 Once ownership of the building has been secured, an architect is appointed to develop an outline scheme design based on the client's brief. A very broad estimate of cost will be produced at this stage based on current development cost indicators.

3 Early contact with the planning department and Historic England will take place to discuss the outline scheme proposals and to gauge their initial reaction. Planning consultants are then likely to be appointed to prepare and submit a planning application and be involved in any future discussions with the local planning authority officers.

4 A range of specialist consultants are likely to be needed to produce various reports to accompany the planning application. Dependent on the nature of the scheme, these can range from a heritage statement to reports covering asbestos, contamination, flood risk, traffic and parking assessment, a tree survey, conservation works, biodiversity or environmental issues.

5 A civil or structural engineer will be required to survey the mill to assess any structural issues and to make recommendations as to how these can be addressed – for example, designing an internal steel frame to support particular floors where there are load-bearing concerns. The structural engineer will also assess the architect's design proposals to ensure that they are achievable. Mechanical and electrical engineering input will also be required on all aspects of heating, ventilation and lift and electrical service installations.

6 A quantity surveyor will also be retained who will be responsible for cost estimates, project cash flow and advising, if required, on the appropriate form of contract for procuring the construction works. Finally, the quantity surveyor is responsible for producing a tender pack, which traditionally is sent to three contractors who are invited to compete for the contract by providing a price for the specified work.

7 A further member of the professional team may be a commercial property agent responsible for marketing the residential and commercial units created by the scheme. Alternatively, larger-scale developers will undertake this role in house. During the initial phases of the scheme development, the property agents will provide intelligence on likely sale prices, levels of demand, local property market dynamics, marketing campaign proposals etc.

Clearly there is considerable input from a large professional development team prior to reaching the stage where planning permission has been obtained and construction tenders can be issued. In the case of a listed mill, this process could easily take several years. This was not so much of an issue during periods of low inflation; however, building material costs have risen sharply over the last two years, with a shortage of skilled workers and inflationary pressures driving up labour costs. Contractor costs have reflected these pressures, resulting in tender prices often far in excess of those expected by the developer. This means schemes may not go ahead or may need to be modified to achieve savings, resulting in further time delays.

James Wimpenny, CEO of Wimpenny Construction, argues that building contractors should be involved at a much earlier stage of the procurement process rather than at the end point, and should be considered part of the development team providing detailed advice on the practicalities of delivering the scheme. The 'contractor can [also] value-engineer and advise on costs throughout the process to avoid any pitfalls, while identifying site constraints affecting the design, build ability and avoid a horrible surprise when at the end a client is presented with costs twice what they were expecting'.

An architect's perspective

Clearly an architect plays a key role in any mill transformation scheme and can offer a number of insights into the development process.

Urban Splash commissioned David Morley Architects to develop proposals for Velvet Mill – part of the Manningham Mills complex in Bradford. Completed in 2018, the Velvet Mill scheme involved the creation of 190 apartments, including a new two-storey rooftop extension, with stunning roof apartments and 6,500 square feet of flexible community and commercial space (**Fig 5.6**).

Originally built in 1838, the Manningham Mills complex contained the world's largest silk mill, with 27 acres of manufacturing floorspace, and employed nearly 11,000 people at its peak. The whole site covers 18 acres, while 'the Heaton Road frontage, one of the finest examples of Victorian masonry in England, is a quarter of a mile long'.

Fig 5.6 Lister Mills.
Courtesy of Neil Mitchell and David Morley

In 1890 the Manningham Mill strike began and lasted for nearly four months. Following the end of the strike, 10,000 textile workers joined trade unions. This led to the founding of the Bradford Labour Union, which, three years later, saw the formation of the national Independent Labour Party in Bradford.

As with all historic buildings there were a number of major issues which had to be addressed in the architect's plans. The Grade II* listed mill had not been used for over 20 years and was in a poor state of repair, with part of its roof missing.

David Morley emphasised the following points in relation to the Velvet Mill design, many of which provide lessons for other mill developments:

- The commission was awarded following an architectural competition run in accordance with RIBA guidelines. Six architectural practices were invited to submit ideas and were interviewed by a panel of key stakeholders including Urban Splash, English Heritage, Bradford Council and Yorkshire Forward. The competition not only generated exciting creative ideas for the mill but gained the early buy-in of the key partners to the radical design proposals for the roof apartments. The early involvement of the various organisations also enabled the scheme to become a key component of wider plans for the regeneration of Manningham.

- Velvet Mill offered a flexible floorplate with a row of cast iron columns down the centre and large windows which let light deep into the building. The scheme involved the creation of apartments on either side of the building accessed by a central corridor, with the stunning cast iron columns integrated as a striking feature along the length of the corridor.

- Where mills have deep floorplates, natural light and ventilation need to be provided to the core of the building. In the case of Velvet Mill, the creation of a glazed atrium at the building's central lift and stairwell was inserted to provide daylight into the mill. In order to bring daylight into the fifth floor, window recesses were created by punching out the stone between the bold dentils below the cornice.

- In other mills, the introduction of central courtyards as well as atria has been used to provide circulation space and an outlook from the front of apartments, although this can result in much lower gross-to-net ratios (ie, the amount of 'saleable' floorspace is reduced, impacting on a scheme's viability).

- Mills with narrower floorplates are more easily adaptable, as individual townhouses can be created via horizontal subdivision of the mill and accessed by external open or enclosed stairways.

- In the case of Velvet Mill, the building's floor-to-ceiling heights were generous, meaning the windowsills were too high for modern apartments. This offered the opportunity of raising the floor height to accommodate service runs beneath it. In other cases, where floor-to-ceiling heights are particularly large, it may be possible to insert a mezzanine floor, creating additional residential units.

- Insulation measures are an important consideration. Around a third of all heat from a building is lost via a building's walls. Mills were constructed with single-skin stone walls, as opposed to the modern practice of building an additional inner cavity wall, so their thermal retention properties can be poor. Consideration therefore needs to be given to adequately insulating the mill's inner walls, to meet residential standards, without compromising the internal heritage design aesthetic. Likewise, insulation materials also need to be applied to the underside of the mill roof.

- Mills have their own quirks and idiosyncrasies. Every mill has its own character which needs to be respected. In Velvet Mill, the wall thicknesses decrease as the building ascends, meaning the respective floorplate dimensions differ slightly throughout the building (a similar issue was commented on by several other developers in relation to a number of other visited mills). Cast iron columns within Velvet Mill were also found to not be symmetrically aligned, being instead offset to accommodate the line shafts which would have originally run down the centre of the building.

Fig 5.7 New Little Mill, Manchester.

- Roof spaces provide the opportunity to add penthouse apartments, which sell at a premium and greatly improve the viability of the project. When adding new-build elements to an existing mill, such as the Velvet Mill roof apartments, David Morley believes it is better to be as bold as possible and not fudge the new with the old by resorting to bland pastiche enhancements. The prominent landmark position of the building, visible across Bradford, offered the opportunity to make a powerful statement about the renewal of both the building and the area. This was achieved by the radical design for the roof apartments. Buildings such as the Reichstag and Tate Modern are good examples of where the old and new have been effectively brought together (**Fig 5.7**).

- The roof apartments, or 'pods' as they have come to be known, also offered the chance to utilise new technologies to create innovative designs – something it was felt mill owner and inventor Samuel Lister would have approved of. The pods were assembled in a factory using state-of-the-art computer cutting technology, which enabled complex shapes to be created from recycled timber. The component parts were then mounted onto a steel framework to produce a series of cassettes which were winched onto the roof, assembled and then clad in zinc.

- Restoration of mills can cost up to 40% more than new-build residential schemes. According to David Morley, in order for many schemes to stack up in areas with low property value, some form of gap funding is likely to be required. In addition, contributions required by local authorities towards affordable housing and local infrastructure may also need to be greatly reduced or waived.

- Accommodating on-site resident and business tenant car parking can be a major issue when planning the development of a mill. Velvet Mill had the advantage of a former lake on the site which historically provided water for the mill steam engines. This provided the opportunity of creating an underground car park with a piazza above bounded by the Velvet and Silk mills. In other cases where site constraints or flooding concerns necessitate car parking on the ground floor, this will also obviously reduce the number of apartments which can be created and the resultant financial return. Many mill renovation schemes have created car parks by demolishing adjoining weaving sheds which have limited architectural and heritage value. A further consideration for developers is the increasing expectation that electric vehicle charge point infrastructure will now be integrated into car park provision.

- The renovation of mills helps meet sustainability goals given the amount of embodied carbon involved in creating new buildings as opposed to renovating existing property stock. The thermal mass of mills also means they are a pleasant temperature, being relatively warm in winter and cool in summer (although office tenants may need to be convinced, given the expectation that air conditioning will be provided in newly refurbished office units).

Velvet Mill is now home to a number of community organisations and businesses; according to one tenant, 'It's a pleasure to work in such an iconic building that brings so much of Bradford's rich history back to life'. However, much of the site has still to be developed. A master plan has been produced for the area, but new uses need to be introduced and considerable investment is still needed to create a critical mass to complete the regeneration process.

Public-sector agency perspectives

When working to deliver a mill renovation scheme, a developer works closely with a wide variety of statutory and non-statutory agencies. It is important to consider their perspective and insights. However, before examining the role of the public sector in facilitating mill regeneration schemes, it is first worth considering the Shrewsbury Flaxmill Maltings as a case study. The mill has received the largest-ever Heritage Lottery grant of £20.7 million, so can be used as an indicator of what makes an exemplar project from the perspective of a range of public agencies.

Shrewsbury Flaxmill Maltings case study

Background

Shrewsbury Flaxmill Maltings was the first purpose-built iron-framed building in the world. In 1796 John Marshall, in partnership with Thomas and Benjamin Benyon and Charles Bage, commissioned the building to be constructed at Ditherington near Shrewsbury. Charles Bage developed a unique design utilising iron technology expertise and skills available in Shropshire derived from work on previous building projects such as Ironbridge.

The site has grown and been repurposed and adapted many times. It was a maltings from 1897 to 1987 and a temporary army barracks during the Second World War. Three successive developers failed to realise their proposals for the site. As a last resort, in 2005 Historic England, as English Heritage until 2015, compulsorily purchased the building, which by then was disused and derelict.

In 2022 the Shrewsbury Flaxmill Maltings opened to the public, offering a visitor museum, café, education workshops, museum shop, and office workspace. Housing will also be built on the site in future years.

Securing public investment

Shrewsbury Flaxmill Maltings (**Figs 5.8** and **5.9**) has received the largest-ever Heritage Lottery Fund grant, £20.7 million, to help finance its renovation. Work started in June 2017 and was completed in March 2023. It is interesting to examine the scheme from a grant funder's perspective to consider the factors which have enabled the mill to secure such levels of public investment. Are there lessons for other mill renovation schemes requiring major public-sector support?

Based on discussions with the project staff, it appears that the following elements were key to the success of the scheme:

- **Uniqueness**. The building is the world's first iron-frame building and is marketed as 'the grandparent to skyscrapers'. At a time when there is intense competition for resources, it is essential to be able to differentiate a project by demonstrating its major importance and contribution to industrial heritage, architecture and social history.

- **Public ownership**. The mill had to be either in or capable of being brought into public ownership to secure the future of the scheme given the five-year renovation timeframe. Historic England compulsory purchased the building in 2005, effectively safeguarding the site for a number of years prior to a funding package being assembled. Historic England held the risk and incurred considerable expenditure securing the site while a scheme was developed, partners recruited and funding obtained. A project champion is essential to 'fly the flag', lobby, and engage other public-sector partners at a senior level.

- **An engaged local authority**. A local council who has been 'in it for the long term' and has maintained the mill renovation as a major priority over many years until such time as funding opportunities became available.

- **Community engagement**. An active local pressure group, The Friends of the Flaxmill Maltings, had articulated local public interest and concern about a potentially lost landmark and campaigned for the mill to be restored.

- **Senior-level champions**. Influential figures, for example within Historic England, with a connection, commitment or knowledge of the building.

- **Availability of gap funding**. The lottery funding was the key to unlocking the future redevelopment of the mill project after Historic England bought the collection of buildings as a purchaser of last resort in 2005. Other public-sector bodies have also contributed significant funding for maintenance and ongoing management of the project. In addition to lottery funding, Historic England raised £1 million through public and private donations towards the main mill restoration.

- **Bid-writing expertise**. Access to skilled staff who could build and co-ordinate a complex funding package – in this case Heritage Lottery, European funding, Shropshire Council and The Marches LEP.

- **Skilled project manager(s)** who can align differing and sometimes competing interested parties within the development timeframe – preservation groups, archaeologists, building contractors, architects, structural engineers and funders.

- **Differing outcomes** for different partners. Public-sector agencies often have different funding priorities and require different outputs to justify their contributions. Outcomes generated by the project ranged from the preservation of a historic building on the Heritage at Risk Register, 300 training places, 350 jobs, volunteer opportunities, creation of workspace employment units, increased tourist visitor numbers, enhanced civic pride, community education and GVA (gross value added) metrics. It is a time-consuming and difficult task to knit together a range of funding bids and deliver outputs which meet the differing priorities of multiple partners.

- **Experienced architects** able to deal with the scale, challenges and complexity of a unique restoration project. An ability to incorporate flexibility in the design of a building which will have a further 300 years of life but whose future uses are largely unknown.

- **Local construction skills**. Availability of local high-level building and professional skills. For many, working on the project has been career defining and enhancing.

- **Communication strategy**. An effective and proactive communication strategy to engage and inform the wider public, which has included telling the stories of local people who have a connection to the mill.

Fig 5.8 Shrewsbury Flaxmill Maltings.

Fig 5.9 Interpretation displays, Shrewsbury Flaxmill Maltings.

Few schemes will be able to meet all of these criteria, but it is interesting to see how the project has been developed to provide different outcomes and outputs needed to meet the requirements of the respective funding bodies resulting in a mill scheme with a £28 million net project value. The importance of garnering local support and ongoing community engagement is also a factor which many scheme proponents ignore or make only token efforts to secure. The project has transformed the main mill building and landmark site. However, other parts of the mill complex still require restoration and further funding will need to be secured to enable future phases of the project to be undertaken.

Historic England

Historic England is the government's statutory adviser on the historic environment and works to preserve and list buildings with significant heritage value. Historic England also has a wider role 'championing historic places and helping people to understand, value and care for them'.

The activities of Historic England can be broadly split between supporting and assessing individual schemes and work on strategic policy.

Individual mill planning applications

Historic England is a statutory consultee in relation to planning applications involving the redevelopment or demolition of a mill that is a listed building or has significant architectural merit. In practice, Historic England may become involved at the pre-application stage, providing advice to both developers or their planning agents and the local planning authority determining the application.

Historic England can draw on a range of in-house specialists such as structural engineers accredited in conservation work, mechanical and electrical engineers, urban designers, an economic appraisal team, climate change advisors etc. Such specialists provide a limited amount of free advice and information, or alternatively developers can commission a bespoke package of expertise from across the range of Historic England specialisms.

The starting point for any mill project is to discuss the future options for the building and their respective viability. More-established developers with experience of mill regeneration schemes will usually have worked-up proposals based on tried-and-tested models. In such cases an assessment will be made by Historic England as to whether the outline proposals are a good fit in relation to the overall heritage significance of the building.

In other cases, mill owners or developers can be at an early stage in their thinking and want to take soundings to see what might be possible from a planning and heritage perspective. In instances where large-scale mills or extensive sites are involved, a master plan may need to be commissioned to provide a framework for a long-term phased incremental development programme. Historic England has limited grant funding but can, in certain circumstances, contribute to master planning exercises, options appraisals and viability assessments to help 'de-risk' sites and provide the confidence to bring forward mill investment schemes. Temple Works in Leeds is an example of a historically important collection of buildings which need to be preserved and repurposed but which have major structural issues. The extensive site has many challenges, and a range of options will need to be assessed to determine potential future uses and their implications for development phasing and overall timescale.

In instances where developers are intent on mill demolition, Historic England's role will be to determine if the building is structurally sound and in good condition and evaluate the developer's viability assumptions. This is an area where most friction arises, with developers often wanting to clear mill sites and replace them with high-density new-build schemes. In such cases there may be protracted negotiations as to how much of the site will be retained and which buildings should be refurbished rather than demolished. If Historic England can demonstrate that a mill is in good structural condition and that viability assessments show that retention is financially feasible, this provides evidence to support the refusal of a planning application and any subsequent appeal.

Heritage statements must be submitted with the planning application if a scheme relates to a listed building or is in a conservation area. In other cases, it is at the discretion of local authorities as to whether a heritage statement is required. Heritage statements give an indication of the significance of the building, how it has evolved over time and its context within the local area. Such assessments establish the relative significance of the building and are taken into account by the local planning authority when reaching a decision as to whether a scheme should receive planning consent.

Historic England can also offer small-scale capacity-building grants to both private-sector and not-for-profit groups such as the Leigh Building Preservation Trust for works at Leigh Spinners Mill. The criteria for support

Fig 5.10 Tileyard North, Wakefield.

are based on 'need, opportunity and deliverability' and the potential outcomes for both the building and local community. Mill buildings which are listed at either Grade I or Grade II* and with significant heritage value are likely to be prioritised.

One issue is that, somewhat surprisingly, in many cases where listed mills are at risk it is unclear who is the building owner. Where buildings have changed hands multiple times and owning companies gone out of business, it can be very difficult to undertake action, given it is not possible to identify who has ultimate responsibility for the upkeep of a specific mill.

Strategic and campaigning role

Historic England has played a vital wider strategic role in assessing the scale and condition of mills at risk and championing their renovation. This has evolved into an ongoing role in raising public awareness of the untapped potential of vacant mills and lobbying for greater priority to be given to mills at risk of demolition.

This has taken the form of commissioning influential reports such as *Engines of Prosperity* and *Driving Northern Growth* and undertaking marketing campaigns and press briefings to gain a national profile for the issue. Between 2017 and 2018 these exercises generated a surprising amount of positive national publicity and helped to raise the profile of the issue both within many local authorities and Historic England itself. This 'thought leadership' role has clearly been important in helping shape and influence policies at both a national and local level.

Historic England's Mills of the North campaign had also generated significant follow-on activities, with a small number of mill owners given the confidence to bring forward redevelopment schemes and mill strategies being developed for specific localities as previously discussed.

There is also evidence that mills are now being included as key components within both Local Plans and wider area-based regeneration proposals being developed by local authorities seeking government financial support.

A further Historic England campaign is that of calling for the scrapping of VAT, currently charged at 20% on the repair and redevelopment of properties. Many see this as particularly unfair given that VAT on the construction of new-build buildings is zero rated. According to Lord Mendoza, Historic England's chairman, 'It's not a level playing field. It would be such a brilliant thing to be able to have the VAT levels at least at the same level – zero on both – so we encourage the reuse of old buildings which people love.'

Mill demolition

Despite the new-found interest in mills, many are still being demolished or left abandoned.

Beehive Mills in Bolton is a cause célèbre involving the demolition in 2019 of a Grade II listed mill which was structurally sound and of significant heritage value. Despite the 520,000 sq ft mill being located just over a mile from Bolton town centre, the developer successfully argued that local market values were so low as to preclude any future redevelopment of the mill buildings for commercial or residential uses. 'Arndale, the developer, estimated a conversion cost of £52m would leave a £30m loss. In the best-case scenario, Arndale estimated a £13m deficit, and also said that "there is very little demand for flats in the area".'

Consequently, the only viable option was for the mill to be demolished to make way for a new-build residential scheme of 121 properties.

Historic England were unable to contest the application at a public enquiry, as in accordance with planning policies, they could not demonstrate any viable medium-term end uses involving the mill's retention. In the absence of any form of public-sector gap funding, Historic England withdrew its objections and 'despite the historic significance of the buildings and their listed status, local Councillors decided that the need for housing, and the "eyesore" nature of the vacant property, outweighed the heritage value'.

Consequently, the planning application was ultimately approved and demolition works began in 2019.

In the case of ongoing industrial uses, many owners and developers often feel that mill sites are not fit for modern purposes and are 'ill-suited to adaptation or the flexibility required for new and growing businesses'. Existing mill site layouts, especially with courtyards, often have poor access and limited room for heavy goods vehicles to turn, together with limited car parking.

Although there is ongoing developer interest in mills in strong property market areas, the key challenge is now to stimulate developer interest in mill schemes in secondary towns where values are low and schemes remain unviable. In the absence of significant gap funding to enable projects in such areas to achieve viability, the likelihood is that mill schemes will need to be positioned in the context of local regeneration 'place-making' plans, which are often dependent on securing central government funding. A targeted regeneration programme with visible investment in buildings and the public realm will hopefully raise the profile of an area and build confidence to a point where the private sector is prepared to come on board and invest.

Local authority perspective

Planning system

Town planners are often stereotyped in negative terms as being inflexible, bureaucratic and difficult to deal with. In reality, planners and elected councillors play an important role in protecting and enhancing the built environment. Local planning authorities (LPAs) are usually receptive to mill development schemes and collaborative engagement can result in a pragmatic and progressive approach to the redevelopment of historic buildings. It is extremely important to build a relationship with the planning case officers who are responsible for dealing with a mill planning application. One of the frustrations of the planning process can be the time taken to determine an application, an issue which, in many smaller authorities, has been exacerbated by a lack of suitably qualified and experienced planning officers.

As commented on earlier, LPAs' attitudes towards mills and industrial developments have evolved since the comprehensive development approaches of the 1980s when councils would acquire land, demolish buildings and clear sites to attract new investment. Instead, the focus is on developing brownfield sites and preserving, retaining and repurposing buildings as part of mixed-use developments. It is unusual for LPAs to have specific policies for mills – they are invariably dealt with on a case-by-case basis. However, authorities can use their powers to safeguard mills under threat – for example, Leeds City Council has designated a number of conservation areas across the city, with accompanying Article 4 directions. This has the effect of removing permitted development rights, including the ability to demolish buildings with significant heritage value, such as mills and their chimneys, located within the conservation area boundaries. It is usually extremely difficult to get permission to demolish a building which has been listed.

In terms of process, a planning application for a mill development scheme must be accompanied by a detailed heritage statement, usually produced by a specialist

Fig 5.11 Shrewsbury Flaxmill Maltings.

consultant, which provides a clear justification for the approach adopted. This will be reviewed by the local authority conservation team. Their comments and those of consultees such as Historic England, local civic trusts or relevant community organisations will be reflected within the planning officers' report to the council Planning or Development Control Committee of elected councillors with a recommendation as to whether the scheme be approved or rejected.

Planning authorities have in recent years been forced to assume a tax collecting role in relation to securing 'planning gain' developer contributions via Section 106 of the Town and Country Planning Act of 1990 or the Community Infrastructure Levy (CIL).

In simplistic terms, these financial contributions can either be a site-specific contribution, for example funding to connect a new housing development to the road network, or a payment supporting wider public needs such as the provision of affordable social housing.

For substantive schemes, the developer will be required to submit a financial viability assessment as part of the planning application process. The business plan is then assessed by the district valuer to determine an appropriate level of financial contribution. A developer contribution towards affordable homes is based on a scheme's 'residual land value' on completion. This is calculated by taking the project's gross development value (GDV) and subtracting its total costs including construction works, professional fees and a developer profit of about 20%. In the case, say, of a proposed scheme to develop detached houses in a suburban location, in order to gain planning permission, the developer could be asked to contribute a financial amount towards social housing provision elsewhere in the local authority area.

In areas where there is market failure, the LPA has had the ability to negotiate a reduction or waive developer CIL and Section 106 financial contributions, thereby enabling the scheme to achieve viability.

In one case, a developer who was interviewed as part of the research was extremely critical of a local authority for enforcing a substantial CIL payment on their mill scheme, collecting payments which were never subsequently spent on social housing in the area and which remain in the council's coffers. In another case, however, the developer had no knowledge of such a system and was bemused by the question, responding, 'They [the local council] don't have any scheme like that round here. If they did then nothing would get built.' Most local authorities will be aware that burdening individual mill regeneration schemes with Section 106 or CIL payments will mean the schemes will not go ahead (**Fig 5.11**).

In October 2023 the Levelling Up and Regeneration Act received royal assent. The Act introduced a new Infrastructure Levy (IL), replacing Section 106 agreements and CIL payments, as a means to secure developer contributions towards infrastructure and affordable housing. Local authorities are now obligated to impose the Infrastructure Levy on developers, with such mandatory charges being based on the gross development value of a scheme rather than its floorspace. However, provision has been made to enable local authorities to revert to using Section 106 contributions should the Infrastructure Levy fail to provide sufficient funding to meet local needs such as targets for affordable housing. How the new system will operate in practice remains to be seen.

Planners can also undertake other measures such as designing and implementing environmental improvements in areas around mills to enhance the area. Visible signs of investment can generate confidence that an area is 'on the up' and encourage others to also consider further investments. Other interventions can be the production of spatial master plans and design guides.

Spatial master plans

Master plans are an urban design tool which can be used to initiate the process of regenerating a mill site and its surrounding area. Master plans were cited as an example of good practice in the Richard Rogers-led Urban Task Force's *Towards an Urban Renaissance* report: 'Unlike conventional two-dimensional zoning plans the "spatial" masterplan establishes a three-dimensional (visual) framework of buildings and public spaces ... they demonstrate the interrelationship between buildings, spaces and their locality ... [and] provide a vital framework for development.'

An example of a design-led master plan approach is that produced for Brierfield Mill, a 380,000 sq ft building on a seven-acre site which had been vacant for seven years prior to its purchase by Pendle Council. The master plan, undertaken by David Morley Architects, envisages converting the mill to contain apartments, a hotel, restaurants, retail space and a gallery. The building will be renamed 'Northlight' and will overlook the creation of a new marina.

The success of Sunny Bank Mills can be attributed in part to the development and adherence to a master plan by owners John and William Gaunt (**Fig 5.12**).

One of the difficulties of assembling and publicising master plans is the need to talk up and excite people about the transformation of an area when there is complete ambiguity as to if, when and how the proposed developments will take place and be financed.

On the positive side, master plans can demonstrate civic leadership and kick-start the regeneration process. They can generate creative new ideas that show how buildings and derelict areas can be re-invented and given new life. They send out strong signals to local people and public- and private-sector funders that an area is being prioritised by the leadership of a local authority who will coordinate their powers and resources to bring about change. They can give confidence to developers and be the basis for recruiting partners needed to assemble a package of public and private investment to deliver the ambitions of the plan. They can also temper the aspirations of specific landowners who may have unrealistic expectations regarding the future uses and potential end values of their sites.

On the downside, where master plans have not worked, or in some cases actually hampered development, has been where

Fig 5.12 Sunny Bank Mills, Farsley.

1. buildings or sites needed to deliver the master plan are not in the ownership of the local authority or its development partners prior to the master plan's publication. There are examples of sites not being secured and the publicity around a master plan resulting in landowners having heightened and often unrealistic expectations as to the value of their property assets, making it difficult to progress the scheme.
2. master plans have been independently commissioned by arms-length joint-venture companies, owned by local authorities and development partners, who have not prepared the ground sufficiently to gain the alignment and buy-in of key individuals such as senior planning department officials or local councillors, to the master plan process and its subsequent proposals.
3. effective and honest communication has not taken place with local residents who either may be fearful of the impacts of gentrification they believe will result from the master plan proposals or who have had their expectations raised that changes are imminent when the delivery of the master plan concepts will take many years to achieve.

Design guides

Design guides are used by LPAs to provide illustrative ideas as to the type of design treatments required for the physical development of a site or area. The *Pendle Textile Mills Design Code* will be a planning tool aimed at promoting high-quality design and good conservation practice for historic textile mills. The project will undertake a number of in-depth case studies of up to 93 textile mills, including those in Brierfield, Colne, Nelson and Barnoldswick.

The interviewed developers were positive about the idea of design guides, primarily from the point of local authorities identifying and promoting potential scheme opportunities via the case study exercises.

Enforcement action

Councils can act, when they see their local heritage assets falling into disrepair, by serving owners with enforcement notices to repair their buildings. A final sanction may be to threaten the owner with the compulsory purchase of the building, although few local authorities seem prepared to go down this road due to both the legal and purchase costs of enforcing a mill compulsory purchase order and uncertainties as to what to do with the building once it is in local authority ownership.

Other public-sector support

Clearly, local authorities and economic development and regeneration agencies have had their budgets greatly reduced by austerity and central government cost cutting. Gone are the days of the Blair government when regional development agencies had access to substantial central government and European structural funds to support property-led regeneration schemes. Such a fiscal environment has been replaced by schemes such as the Levelling Up Fund, where resources are allocated on the basis of competitive bids and political expediency. However, although there are now fewer sources of funding, there is usually some form of financial investment support that astute developers can access – for example the Merseyside Pension 'Catalyst' Fund loan investment being used to develop Heap Mills, Liverpool.

The public sector's ability to support mill schemes will therefore vary over time according to the availability or otherwise of financial resources. The level of potential support for a mill development can be regarded as an incremental ladder of engagement ranging from low to high interventions – see diagram.

Where public sector organisations position themselves on the ladder will be dependent on resources and the levels of political and senior officer ambition and commitment.

Public sector support ladder

High Intervention

- Public sector acts as developer in its own right via a publicly owned development vehicle. Secures partner support and financial investments. Acquires mills at risk to bring into public ownership pending assembly of a funding package.
- Equity investment – public-sector partner in a joint venture with private-sector partner(s). Considers acting as a guarantor for space or enters into a pre-let arrangement for commercial spaces created by a mill redevelopment.

Medium Intervention

- Creation of mill support investment funds including gap funding to enable a scheme to achieve viability.
- Grants for abnormal costs such as contamination or flood alleviation measures.
- Mill area environmental improvement schemes – secure funding and delivery.
- Proactive and creative support through the planning system for individual schemes together with wider policy measures to safeguard mills. Support for schemes by flexibility over Section 106 and CIL contributions. Protects mills using measures such as Article 4 and conservation area status.
- Small-scale feasibility grant contributions.

Low Intervention

- Develop specific project proposals ready for when funding sources become available.
- Appoint a dedicated project manager to lead on taking forward a mills strategy and co-ordinating a partner task and finish group.
- Commissioning of a mills audit and development strategy – assess mills at risk and assemble priorities for intervention.
- Moral support for individual mill schemes but no financial support.
- General championing role, talking-up the importance of retaining and repurposing mills.

Conditioning House

The Bradford Corporation built Conditioning House in 1902 to provide laboratories for checking the weight, length and condition of worsted cloth. In its heyday, around 70% of all UK-made wool was brought to Conditioning House for testing. Prior to redevelopment, the building had not been in use for 30 years and had fallen into a dilapidated state.

Priestley Homes, led by Nathan Priestley, has undertaken an £18 million regeneration scheme creating 153 modern apartments. The U-shaped structure surrounds a once-open court, with a reinstated glass roof creating a full-height atrium. Ironwork link bridges, connecting the two main mills, have been restored, while the original factory gates, internal doors and ornate stonework have also been retained.

Right Walkways.

Left Gates.

Leigh Spinners Mill

Leigh Spinners Mill was one of the largest cotton-spinning mills built in Britain. According to the Leigh Building Preservation Trust, 'with its neo-Baroque influenced architecture, staircased towers and engine houses it is one of the most complete mills still intact in Greater Manchester'.[57]

The Grade II* listed mill was built by local entrepreneurs John Horrocks and Edward Crowther. The east section, comprising the six-storey mill, boiler house and chimney stack, was constructed in 1913 and the matching western section, containing Mill 2, was completed in 1925.

The Leigh Building Preservation Trust Ltd was formed in 2013 to restore the historic Yates & Thom cross-compound mill steam engines and engine house. By January 2019, the Trust had raised sufficient funds to undertake extensive roof repairs, and further works have since been undertaken to the eastern, western and northern sides, where extensions have been erected to create new business space.

The Preservation Trust has secured leases on the mills and created a public heritage centre featuring the renovated steam engines. Tenants within the mill also include a cinema, computer museum, gym, café, archery centre, boxing club, music studio and logistics company. The manufacture of carpet and artificial turf also still occurs in part of the mill complex.

Leigh Spinners Mill.

Restored steam engine,
Leigh Spinners Mill.

Black Dyke Mills

Following the success of the family-run Cannon Mill in Bradford, in 1835 John Foster commissioned the construction of a new mill at Black Dykes Farm near Queensbury. Foster successfully experimented with new fabrics, including the use of alpaca and mohair and re-invested profits in developing the mill site. Black Dyke Mills became a pioneering factory incorporating power looms, together with the establishment of its own fire service and gasworks which supplied both the village and the mill. Later developments included the construction of reservoirs to provide the mill with its own water supply. Ultimately the mill evolved to become an integrated manufacturing complex where yarn was spun, woven and dyed and fine-quality worsted cloth produced.

The decline of the West Yorkshire wool and textiles industries led to the eventual closure of the mill in 1989. The current owners, the Lowry Partnership, have since refurbished parts of the mill and let space to a range of tenants including a boxing gym, The Bike Mill, The Marshall's Music School, Mpika (a charity shop that raises money for an African village), and Hovercart Mania, Yorkshire's first indoor electric racing track. Currently around 90% of the floorspace is let, and work is underway on refurbishing vacant space to accommodate a range of new business, leisure and heritage uses.

The mills have had a long historical association with music, ever since 1855 when John Foster helped found the Black Dyke Mills Band, which became one of the world's best-known brass bands. More recently, the Black Dyke Mills Heritage Venue is a live music and community space located in the Shed Mill. The venue is run and managed entirely by volunteers and is a showcase for top-quality grassroots musicians.

Heritage Venue.

Chimney, Black Dyke Mills.

Black Dyke Mills.

Redbrick Mill

Victoria Mill was originally a steam-powered woollen mill built in Batley in the 1860s. By 1900 the site had evolved, with production divided between the main mill and associated sheds for weaving, finishing and dyeing. Fifteen years later, the site housed a large rag warehouse and grinding shed turning 'shoddy' into new, lower-grade textiles.

Redbrick Mill was launched in 2000 by Chris Bullus, mill owner, and Stephen Battye, a local textile entrepreneur, with the ambition to create a major high-end retail destination. Victoria Mill was restored in a sympathetic and imaginative manner, including the installation of escalators and passenger lifts linking the four floors.

According to Battye, founder of Skopos, 'We took a building worth practically nothing and turned it into a magnet for all kinds of firms who would otherwise not be in this part of West Yorkshire'.[58]

Redbrick Mill is now one of the north's premier shopping destinations, containing a number of independent interiors brands together with a restaurant and other visitor facilities.

Design.

Right and below
Mill interior.

Below right
Redbrick Mill façade.

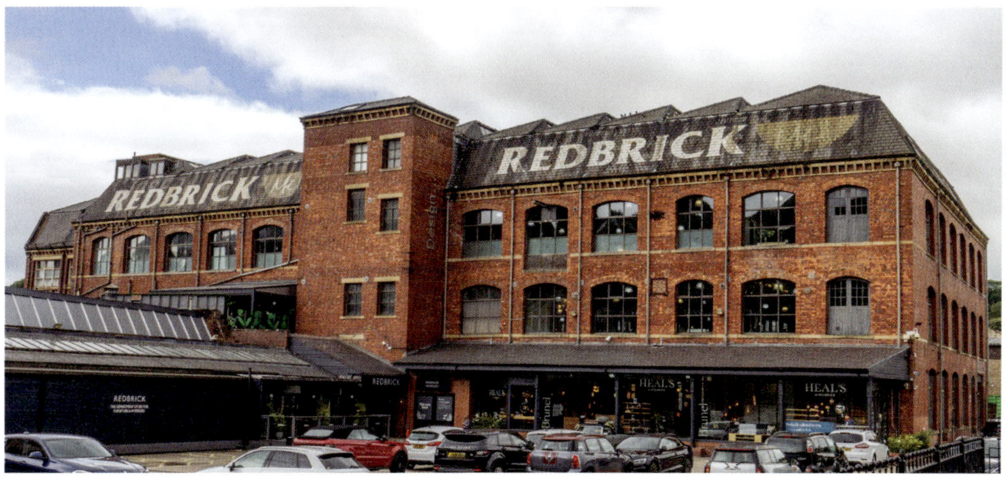

Legrams Mill

Legrams Mill in Bradford was built in 1873 for loom manufacturer George Hodgson as an integrated mill with combing shed, mill, weaving shed and warehouse. The mill architects were the renowned Lockwood and Mawson responsible for many of Bradford's major buildings. Their Italianate-style design for Legrams Mill features belvedere towers either side of the building, similar to those incorporated in their plans for Salts Mill.

After 1973 the mill became partly divided into industrial units. Legrams Mill was awarded a Grade II listing in 1983.

Browntree Properties Limited has since acquired the building and converted the vacant fourth floor into 23 student flats and a common room. All works have been completed and the building is fully occupied, providing accommodation for a wedding gift shop, banqueting suite and grill restaurant.

6

The way forward: A future approach

During work on the *Mills Transformed* project, it has been inspiring to see how much progress has been made in repurposing previously abandoned textile mills at the heart of local communities. Mills have transitioned from being unwanted relics of a bygone industrial age to repurposed functional modern buildings providing attractive living and working environments. Back in the 1980s, when widespread closures took place across the textile industry resulting in a substantial stock of empty buildings, it would have been inconceivable that mills in places such as Ancoats or in the heart of Leeds city centre would become valuable, sought-after real estate properties providing high-end 'city-living' apartments. Much of this has been due to the vision, persistence and perseverance of a small group of individuals who have had to develop new skills to bring about such mill transformations. These individuals should be celebrated for their achievements in preserving and repurposing great swathes of our industrial heritage.

Although substantial progress has been made in recognising the heritage value of mills and delivering successful renovation schemes, we are only part way into the process. Given there are still, at the last count, more than 680 vacant or underutilised mills across Yorkshire and Lancashire alone, considerable work is still required to save and repurpose mills, many of which are close to a state of terminal disrepair.

What is apparent is an increasing divide between cities and towns across northern England due to the influence of localised property markets. Any vacant mill in Manchester city centre will now be acquired and redeveloped by the private sector as a matter of course due to the high end-values, ability to attract investors and strong demand for apartments and commercial space. However, in Bolton, property values are so low as to make, in the case of the Beehive Mill, a conversion scheme unviable, resulting to the demolition of a Grade II listed mill. Similarly, across the Pennines in Leeds, a dynamic property market will drive investment into former mill buildings whereas there is little developer interest in similar properties in nearby West Yorkshire towns.

The question is therefore how to kick-start a second wave of mill regeneration where there is market failure and little if any interest from the private sector. Is there anything that can be done and if so who should lead? I would argue that ultimately leadership has to come from the local authorities within whose boundaries vacant mills are located. Local authorities have an electoral mandate, are closer to the ground, understand the challenges better and have leverage as the designated local planning authority. If local authorities do not take on this role, it is difficult to see who else will.

At a time when local authority budgets have been slashed to the bone it is very easy for a mindset to prevail that nothing much can be done as councils do not have the scale of resources needed to initiate major mill regeneration projects in their area. However, as has been shown previously in the Public Sector Support Ladder (Chapter 5), there is a wide range of interventions which local authorities can take according to the availability of resources at any given point in time. Finding funding will always be difficult, but is in no way impossible – grant schemes come and go, but there is always something available to bid for.

So, why is progress slow or in some areas non-existent? Can anything be done at a practical level to kick-start mill regeneration schemes? Based on the conversations with many of the mill renovators the answer is a strong 'yes', but this will require leadership and commitment at a senior level from councils over a number of years.

The following is a 'Mills Manifesto' listing a number of suggestions as to what practical actions can be taken at a local level.

1. Appoint a dedicated project manager

At the outset, someone needs to be given responsibility to coordinate action across a local authority, otherwise nothing will happen. A dedicated project manager needs to be identified from within the council who, as part of their work, can lead on the authority's mill regeneration activities.

Key to the success of any group will be to ensure cross-authority participation and commitment, especially from relevant planning officers and economic development officers who are often based in separate divisions with limited lines of communication between them.

In the first instance, the project manager should convene a senior-level officer task group to achieve corporate buy-in and ideas as to what practical steps can be taken to catalyse local mill regeneration.

2. Produce a mills strategy

A first step may be to produce a mills strategy for the local authority, overseen by members of the officer task group, but with other key organisations such as Historic England invited to participate in its drafting.

The mere act of embarking on the production of a district-wide mills plan demonstrates a recognition of the problem and a commitment to doing something about it. Such a strategy could be commissioned using external consultants, with financial support from local regeneration or public agencies, or could be a relatively simple document produced in house by council officers.

Such a plan needs to include an audit to identify the number of vacant mills in the district, their physical state of repair, ownership, and current development plans if any, and culminate in a prioritisation of vacant mills based on their contribution to both providing housing and employment space and their potential to be a catalyst for wider neighbourhood regeneration.

Having such a strategy, with senior councillor backing, sends out a strong message both internally and externally, puts down a marker that redundant mills are a priority, and will make it far easier to stimulate the interest of potential private-sector partners.

3. Delivery plan

The mills strategy needs to have an associated delivery plan, summarising actions, outcomes, individual responsibilities and timescales. Without such a delivery plan there is a danger that the council's mills strategy loses momentum and become a pointless paper exercise. The task group would review the delivery plan, at each of its meetings, to assess and chase progress.

Having produced a mills strategy, which has focused on one or two mill priority targets, an important next step is for the local authority to consider what actions it can itself initially take, followed by those where it will need help from other partners.

4. Review local planning authority role

A useful starting point may be for a local authority to consider ways in which its planning authority function can be transitioned from a regulatory to an enabling role. All too often the planners are considered as an afterthought when it comes to councils developing their own regeneration strategies.

A wide range of interventions might be possible, such as

- Following the example of Leeds City Council in designating a number of conservation areas across a city or town, with accompanying Article 4 directions making it very difficult to demolish buildings with heritage value in the designated areas.

- Consider enforcement action to force owners to undertake remedial measures where the condition of a listed mill is of concern.

- Assess the value of designing and implementing environmental improvements around mills to enhance the appearance of an area. Visible signs of investment can generate confidence that an area is 'on the up' and encourage others to also consider further investments. Funding for such works could form part of a package to local funding bodies such as Local Enterprise Partnerships.

- Review the council's approach to affordable housing contributions to see if a more innovative and flexible approach can be adopted and whether lessons can be learnt from other progressive local authorities such as Manchester City Council.

5. Investment plan

A key role for the task group is to identify funding sources and seek to embed mills into any future council regeneration funding bids.

It may be that there are no immediate opportunities, but the example of the Shrewsbury Flaxmill Maltings is that this is a long-term game and that substantial gap funding can be achieved by carefully packaging bids to achieve the different aims of multiple agencies such as the Heritage Lottery Fund, combined authorities, Local Enterprise Partnerships etc.

Depending on its level of ambition, a local authority may want to consider the establishment of a special-purpose development vehicle to lead on its mill regeneration development plans. The local authority would have a stake in such a company, along with a number of private-sector partners.

6. Spatial master plans

Having considered internal local authority measures, the next stage would be to undertake discussions with potential partners to see if there is an appetite to develop outline concept plans for one or more of the identified mill priority schemes. Such plans would view the mill(s) in the context of their immediate surrounding areas and would ideally be in the ownership of one of the partner organisations.

As previously mentioned, a design-led spatial master plan visioning exercise for a specific area can provide both a useful visual framework and context for future development. Master plans can be used to change perceptions of an area, excite interest, demonstrate a council's commitment to an area and be used as a marketing tool to attract development partners and investors.

7. Architectural competitions

Where mill development schemes have a potential development partner in place, a more fine-grained action could be the commissioning of an architectural competition. Organised in accordance with RIBA guidelines, architectural competitions can be a vehicle to achieve a high-quality innovative design proposal which will establish a benchmark for both the mill and subsequent development schemes in the locality.

Inviting key public- and private-sector organisations to be involved in designing the brief and commissioning both spatial master plans and/or architectural competitions is an effective way of securing early buy-in and the support of organisations who will have an ongoing role in the scheme's future delivery.

8. Historic England

Historic England has played a highly significant campaigning role highlighting both the condition of mill stock and their potential contribution to wider economic and social objectives. Such work has been vitally important in raising the profile of the issue and stimulating the interest and involvement of a wide range of organisations. Historic England has a number of Heritage at Risk teams who focus on rescuing buildings to the point where they can be removed from the Heritage at Risk Register. Historic England has also had a pump-priming role helping joint-fund local authority mill strategies and small-scale feasibility studies, while also providing access to a wide range of technical conservation skills and expertise.

It is important that Historic England maintain this national campaigning role, complementing work happening at a local level, into a second wave of mill regeneration schemes in northern towns.

9. Regional economic development agencies and LEPs

Economic development agencies also have a key role to play and should acknowledge the potential role vacant mills can play in creating jobs and housing units. They have the ability to support schemes through gap funding and loans and to provide initial joint funding for mill strategies, feasibility studies etc. An important first step is to embed mill programmes within their wider economic strategies and funding negotiations with central government.

As we have seen, not-for-profit groups have been instrumental in successfully campaigning for the preservation of mills and in some cases have ultimately taken on the management of renovated mills. Such groups need the support of such funding agencies in terms of access to small grants to undertake early-stage project studies and fund small capital investment, together with marketing and communication materials to achieve wider community engagement.

10. Mill regeneration dissemination and networks

During the interviews with mill renovators, a number of requests were received for information and contacts relating to other mill schemes. There seemed to be a strong interest in visiting and networking with other counterpart mill owners and developers to compare experiences and gain insights. There would appear to be scope for forming an informal information-sharing network which would

- celebrate the achievements of mill renovators
- share good practice in mill restoration works
- campaign to maintain the profile of mills as a key local and national priority.

This is just a brief list of potential interventions – there are no doubt many more – but the central message is that there is no shortage of actions that can be taken to bring forward further projects to preserve and repurpose mills for them to continue to be a unique feature of our local landscapes.

Acknowledgements

Special thanks to

- All at Bingley Camera Club, for their support, advice and inspiration. A special mention for Terry Roberts.
- All the numerous mill developers who made time to see me including: William and John Gaunt, Richard and Barbara Trainer, Ben Clay, Janet and John Emanuel, Ian and Nicola Kellett, Charles Moran, Debbie Duke, Neil McNair, Jon and June Barrow, Guy Taylor, Adam Higgins, Ivan Moorhouse, Brian O'Connell, Richard Hall and Paul Meikle-Janney.
- Thanks also to Tony Clegg, Charles Smith, David Morley, Heritage Trust for the North West, Castleford Heritage Trust, Dixons Sixth Form Academy, Dan and the team at Dandelion Café, Laura Horsley and Mary Horsley who first suggested a book.
- John Hudson, Matt Wilson, Auriol Griffith-Jones and Sarah Enticknap.
- Bradford Museums Photo Archive for permitting use of the image on p 69.
- Bradford District Museums and Galleries for hosting an exhibition of the author's photographs in 2024–25 at Bradford Industrial Museum.
- David Morley Architects for financial support towards publication.

Photography

All photographs taken by Neil Horsley unless otherwise stated.

Contact and further information

For further information about the Mills Transformed project, to purchase copies of the images or if you have suggestions of mills to be documented please contact Neil via the contacts page of **www.mills-transformed.com**

Mills Transformed

References

Binney, M, Fitzgerald, R, Langenbach, R, and Powell, K 1979 *Satanic Mills*. SAVE Britain's Heritage

Bradford Heritage Recording Unit 1994 *Here to Stay, Bradford's South Asian Communities*. Bradford: Bradford Art Museums and Libraries Service

Brown, Mark 2023 'Dewsbury in Yorkshire Recognised as "Greenest Town" of the 1800s'. *The Guardian*, 8 September.

Brunskill, R W 1971 *Illustrated Handbook of Vernacular Architecture.* London: Faber and Faber

Burgess, Jon 1998 *Lockwood and Mawson of Bradford and London*. PhD thesis, DeMontfort University, Leicester

Cronshaw, Jon 2015 'Temple Works: The Most Extreme Venue in Leeds'. Leeds Art Scene. https://artyorkshire.wordpress.com/2013/05/02/temple-works-the-most-extreme-venue-in-leeds/comment-page-1/ (accessed 19 October 2015)

Dowle, Jayne 2024 'Why Leeds is a Northern Star'. *Sunday Times*, 14 April

Emanuel, Susan 2012 *Hewenden Mill Cottages*. www.blurb.com/b/4754176-hewenden-mill-cottages?ebook=446833

Firth, Gary 1987 'Introduction' *in* Ian Beesley, *Through the Mill*. Skipton: Dalesman

Florida, Richard 2012 *The Rise of the Creative Class*. New York: Basic

Gibson Mill Building Design Guide (National Trust 2005), as quoted in Lewis, Hywel, and Atkinson, Christopher 2019 *An Archaeological Woodland Survey Celebrating Our Woodland Heritage*, report commissioned by Pennine Prospects. Report No: PP30-160419. https://nationaltrusthbsmr.esdm.co.uk/LLWS/LLFiles/219563/original_219563.pdf

Giles, Colum, and Goodall, Ian H 1992 *Yorkshire Textile Mills: The Building of the Yorkshire Textile Industry 1770–1930.* London: HMSO

Goddard, Christopher, and Gray, Michael 2022 *The Sowerby Bridge Industrial Heritage Walk*. Calderdale Industrial Museum Association

Greenhalf, Jim 1997 *Salt and Silver: A Story of Hope*. Bradford: Bradford Libraries

Griffiths, Sian, and Al-Othman, Hannah 2023 'Heartbreak over Crooked House "Shows How Much We Care about Heritage"'. *Sunday Times*, 13 August

Hall, David 2006 *Fred: The Definitive Biography of Fred Dibnah*. London: Bantam

Heaton, Andrew *Heatons of Worth*. The author. www.heatonfamilyonline.com/heatonsofworth.html

Historic England 2018 *Mills – Introductions to Heritage Assets*. Swindon: Historic England. https://historicengland.org.uk/images-books/publications/iha-mills/heag212-mills/

Historic England 2023 *Stories in Stone. Timeline for Bradford's Migration History*. https://historicengland.org.uk/services-skills/education/teaching-activities/stories-in-stone-timeline-of-bradford/

Historic England, Cushman & Wakefield, and Lathams 2016 *Engines of Prosperity: New Uses for Old Mills*. Swindon: Historic England. https://historicengland.org.uk/images-books/publications/engines-of-prosperity-new-uses-old-mills/

Historic England, Cushman & Wakefield, and Lathams 2021 *Driving Northern Growth Through Repurposing Historic Mills*. Swindon: Historic England. https://historicengland.org.uk/images-books/publications/driving-northern-growth-repurposing-mills/

Huddleston, Yvette 2023 'Still Life Long After the Looms Fell Silent'. *Yorkshire Post* Magazine, 25 March. www.pressreader.com/uk/yorkshire-post-yp-magazine/20230325/281668259225526

Keighley, Mark 1990 *A Fabric Huge – The Story of Listers*. London: James & James

Middleton-Pugh, Jessica 2017 'Outrage and Elation as Bolton Listed Mill Demolition Looks Likely'. Place North West, 27 September. www.placenorthwest.co.uk/outrage-and-elation-as-bolton-listed-mill-demolition-looks-likely/

Morley, Paul 2021 *From Manchester with Love*. London: Faber

Newton, Grace 2019 'This is Why there are So Many Fires at Mills in Yorkshire'. *Yorkshire Post*, 20 March. www.yorkshirepost.co.uk/news/transport/fire-mill-1758023

Oldham Mills Strategy 2021 ELG Heritage and ELG Planning. Report commissioned by Historic England and Oldham Council. www.oldham.gov.uk/downloads/file/7192/oldham_mill_strategy_2021

Olusoga, David, and Backe-Hansen, Melanie 2020 *A House Through Time*. London: Picador

Redhead, N 2017 *Historic Mills of Greater Manchester, Survey and Heritage Audit*. Swindon: Historic England. https://historicengland.org.uk/images-books/publications/historic-textile-mills-greater-manchester/greater-manchester-textile-mills-survey-exec-summary /

Reid, Laura 2020 'Meet the Developer Weaving a Creative Future for Wakefield's Rutland Mills'. *Yorkshire Post*, 16 March. www.yorkshirepost.co.uk/business/meet-the-developer-weaving-a-creative-future-for-wakefields-rutland-mills-2453886

Smith, Tim, and Howarth, Olive 2006 *Textile Voices. A Century of Mill Life*. Bradford Recording Heritage Unit

Timan, Joseph 2019 'Bolton's Beehive Mills Demolition for New Development Begins'. *Bolton News*, 5 September. www.theboltonnews.co.uk/news/17880772.boltons-beehive-mills-demolition-new-development-begins/

Urban Task Force 1999 *Towards a Strong Urban Renaissance*. London: Spon

Wainwright, Martin 2011 'Trouble at Mill: Recession Brings Renewed Threat of Bulldozers'. *The Guardian*, 21 March.

Williams, Mike, with Farnie, D A 1992 *Cotton Mills in Greater Manchester*. Preston: Carnegie

Young, Chris 2023 'Keighley Mill Could Be Flattened to Make Way for Development'. *Telegraph and Argus*, 14 March. www.thetelegraphandargus.co.uk/news/23383539.keighley-mill-flattened-make-way-development/

Endnotes

1 'Highly Respected Writer Talks about Being an Ambassador for the "Living Landscape" of the South Pennines Park'. South Pennine Park website, 17 September 2021. https://southpenninespark.org/2021/09/17/highly-respected-writer-talks-about-being-an-ambassador-for-the-living-landscape-of-the-south-pennines-park/.

2 Historic England *et al* 2021, p 2.

3 Redhead.

4 Olusoga and Backe-Hansen, p 2.

5 Historic England *et al* 2021, p 2.

6 YouGov poll undertaken for Historic England conducted October 2017.

7 *Manchester Evening News*, 20 November 2017.

8 Brunskill, p 183.

9 *Yorkshire Post*, 26 February 2022.

10 Oldham Mills Strategy.

11 Giles and Goodall, p 20.

12 Ibid, p 132.

13 Ibid.

14 Williams and Farnie, p 1.

15 Ibid, p 17.

16 Keighley, p 19.

17 Williams and Farnie, p 98.

18 Oldham Mills Strategy, pp 46–7.

19 Historic England 2018.

20 Giles and Goodall, p 41.

21 Ibid, p 150.

22 Hall.

23 Giles and Goodall, p 3.

24 Burgess, p 122.

25 Keighley, p 19.

26 Binney *et al*, p 7.

27 Morley, p 291.

28 Olusoga and Backe-Hansen, p 94.

29 Bankfield House Museum display, Halifax, 2023.

30 Goddard and Gray.

31 Greenhalf, p 57.

32 Historic England 2023.

33 Firth.

34 BBC Archive, 'The Future of the Lancashire Cotton Industry', broadcast on Tuesday 10 December 1957.

35 Gibson Mill Building Design Guide, p 22.

36 Binney *et al*.

37 Historic England *et al* 2021, p 2.

38 Historic England *et al* 2016.

39 Oldham Mills Strategy.

40 Report of the Oldham Borough Estates Officer, Andrew Harris, 18 February 1977.

41 Binney *et al*, p 16.

42 Oldham Mills Strategy.

43 Florida.

44 Huddleston.

45 *Yorkshire Times*, 11 April 2023. www.yorkshiretimes.co.uk/article/Sunny-Bank-Mills-Celebrates-Ten-Years-Of-Arts-And-Culture.

46 Reid.

47 Dowle.

48 'My Yorkshire'. William Gaunt interview, *Yorkshire Post*, the magazine, Saturday 26 February 2022.

49 Sir Ernest Hall. Desert Island Discs. BBC broadcast, 1 May 1998.

50 Greenhalf, p 75.

51 Ibid, p 78.

52 Greenhalf, p 78.

53 Heaton, p 47.

54 *Yorkshire Post* interview, Saturday 15 January 2022.

55 Emanuel, p 11.

56 http://news.bbc.co.uk/1/hi/england/west_yorkshire/4242784.stm.

57 Interpretation board on display at Leigh Spinners Mill produced by the Leigh Building Preservation Trust.

58 Wainwright.

59 Burgess, p 124.

60 Giles and Goodall, p 30.

61 Ibid, p 91.

62 Brown.

63 Cronshaw, Jon 2015 'Temple Works: The Most Extreme Venue in Leeds'. Leeds Art Scene. https://artyorkshire.wordpress.com/2013/05/02/temple-works-the-most-extreme-venue-in-leeds/comment-page-1/ (retrieved 19 October 2015)

64 Smith and Howarth, p 14.

65 Ibid, p 16.

66 Greenhalf, p 54.

67 Bradford Heritage Recording Unit, p 63.

68 *Yorkshire Post, 26 February 2022.*

69 Newton.

70 West Yorkshire Police, 2022.

Index

Advance Subscribers

The publisher and author are grateful to the following, and others who prefer to remain anonymous, who have aided publication of this book through advance subscriptions. This is much appreciated, and by doing so they have contributed to the awareness and appreciation of mills and the important role they play in our national heritage.

Paul Andrews
Rodney Billings
Colin Cheesman
June Diamond
Nigel Grizzard
Roger Holden
Julia Matheson
Charles Moran
David Morley Architects
Cheryll Roberts
Caroline Walker
Geoffrey Wood
Richard Woolf

About the Author

Neil is a qualified Town Planner with over 40 years' experience in the field of urban regeneration.

Based in West Yorkshire, Neil is a keen walker and photographer who first began documenting mills as a lockdown project.